Lessons ▶ in Numeracy

Barbara Ball Derek Ball

Longman

GCSE INTERMEDIATE

Pearson Education Limited
Edinburgh Gate
Harlow
Essex
CM20 2JE
England and Associated Companies throughout the World

ISBN 0582 47387 X

First published 2001

Designed by Mathematical Composition Setters Ltd, Salisbury, Wiltshire

Printed in the UK by George Over Limited, Rugby

The Publisher's policy is to use paper manufactured from sustainable forests.

Contents

Introduction

Aims and overview

The National Numeracy Strategy defines numeracy as 'proficiency which involves confidence and competence with numbers and measures. It requires an understanding of the number system, a repertoire of computational skills and an inclination and ability to solve number problems in a variety of contexts'. This resource is designed to ensure that students have the numerical knowledge, skills and understanding required for the mathematics being undertaken elsewhere in the mathematics curriculum and indeed in the curriculum of other subjects.

Contents

There is one book for each of the Foundation, Intermediate and Higher tiers of the GCSE specifications. Each book contains 40 stand-alone teacher-led lessons, each consisting of

- lesson objectives
- detailed teacher's notes
- a photocopiable homework sheet (with answers)

and almost all containing

- a photocopiable classwork sheet (with answers).

On the whole the assumption is made that the ideas being taught are likely to have been met before, some of them on several occasions. So, for many lessons, the approach adopted is to enable students to review, consolidate and strengthen their skills and to gain an overview of the topic that will increase their confidence in using it. This resource focuses unashamedly on techniques rather than on the application of these techniques over a wide range of contexts. In particular, 'real-life contexts' are only introduced where they are essential for the understanding of the skill being taught. The aim is for students to hone skills in isolation, so that they can be applied confidently in problem solving and other areas of mathematics.

While reflecting the need for students to understand and have competence with standard written algorithms the course also, wherever possible, encourages students to develop or consolidate a range of mental strategies and common-sense methods of approaching arithmetical situations, rather than having to use a standard written method in circumstances where this is far from efficient or sensible.

This resource covers the Number part of the GCSE specifications in each of the three tiers. Because of the overlap in tiers there is also some overlap in the materials, but this overlap is not extensive.

Each of the 40 lessons can be taught at any time and followed by the homework provided. Although each of the 40 lessons stands alone, the lessons are arranged in a logical order, and the skills developed in one lesson are used in subsequent lessons where they are relevant.

Structure of each lesson

Each stand-alone lesson is designed to last between 45 minutes and an hour, with a follow-up homework of about 30 minutes.

Full notes are provided to support teachers in structuring the approach recommended by the NNS. Each lesson has a three-part structure:

- working interactively
- individual work
- review

The first phase of each lesson involves working interactively, and detailed notes are provided to help with this. The assumption of the resource is that each lesson is going to be taught; this is not a resource that can be used independently of a teacher. The notes are sufficiently detailed to be given to a supply teacher or a teacher who works in the department on an occasional basis.

The approaches suggested for working interactively include the following:

- *Speaking in unison* (e.g. counting in sevens, starting at 9; making 100 (you say 37, they say 63))
- *Individual response* (each student thinking of or writing down the answer; students being invited to volunteer information by putting up their hands; asking an individual student)
- *Explaining and listening* (asking students to come out to the board and explain how they obtained their answer; the teacher explaining a technique on the board)

The second phase of each lesson involves students working individually on relevant questions. Sometimes this phase occurs in one block. In other lessons there are two blocks of individual work interspersed with more interactive working. For this phase a photocopiable classwork sheet is provided for almost all lessons; there are one or two lessons where instead a task for students is described in detail in the lesson notes.

The final phase of each lesson is a review. The teacher can discuss with the class problems they experienced with the classwork sheet, and the teaching notes suggest key strategies to be reviewed, so that students know what the topic is all about.
On the whole, homework sheets are written to mirror the classwork sheets. In this way they provide students with the opportunity to be confident that they will be able to do the work set and to consolidate their understanding of the topic without the support of the teacher.

Answers

Answers to the classwork sheets are included with each set of teacher's notes. Answers to the homework are all together on pages 133–137 at the back of the book.

Calculators and resources

Throughout the lessons the emphasis is on work without a calculator wherever appropriate and certainly wherever this is expected in the GCSE specifications. There are some topics in the Number section of the GCSE specifications which clearly cannot be tackled without a calculator and for these topics a calculator is specified. Each classwork sheet and homework sheet clearly specifies where calculators may or may not be used. At the start of the teacher's notes for each lesson there is either a calculator symbol or a no-calculator symbol or both symbols.

Where both symbols appear, some parts of the topic of the lesson are to be developed without calculators and some parts with calculators.

Calculators are the only equipment required for the lessons, apart from the classwork sheets. Almost all the sheets are designed not to be written on, and so can be re-used.

How to use this resource

There are various ways in which you could use this resource within your school. Each week, one of the 40 lessons could be used, so that the focus is on Number for one lesson each week during Key Stage 4; or sequences of lessons could be used in blocks if, for example, you wanted to spend one or two weeks teaching percentages; or the lessons could be used in one or more blocks for revision of Number.

1 Mental strategies for addition and subtraction

> **LESSON OBJECTIVES**
> ● Develop a range of strategies for mental calculation
> ● Use integer complements to 100 and 1000
> ● Add and subtract numbers mentally

WORKING INTERACTIVELY

● Start with a number, say 36.
Count on in 6s (42, 48, 54, …)
or 30s (66, 96, 126, …)
or 15s (51, 66, 81, 96, …)
or 29s (65, 94, 123, 152, 181, …).
Note patterns that help students to know they have not made a mistake.

● How do students do questions such as 15 + 19 in their heads? Also + 99 and + 199, etc.

● How about additions such as 57 + 26?
(e.g. 57 + 20 = 77 and then 77 + 6; or 50 + 20 = 70 and 7 + 6 = 13).

● Making 100 (you say 37, students say 63, etc.) and 1000. Do lots of each until the response become automatic.

● Making 500 or 800 or 350, etc. in a similar way.

● Start with 459. Count back in 7s.

● Start with 1328. Count back in 20s or 15s.

● Subtracting 19 (subtract 20 and add 1), subtracting 99, 199, etc.

● Other subtractions such as 131 – 57
(e.g. 131 – 50 = 81, 81 – 7 = 74; or 131 – 60 = 71, 71 + 3 = 74).
Give a subtraction like this for students to do and then collect together different methods students used to do it.

INDIVIDUAL WORK

Students work through the classwork sheet.

Review

Mark any classwork and review strategies which appeared problematic in the interactive session.

ANSWERS TO THE CLASSWORK SHEET

1 87, 112, 137, 162, 187, 212, 237, 262, 287, 312
2 434, 415, 396, 377, 358, 339, 320, 301, 282, 263
3 (a) 600 (b) 330 (c) 645 (d) 495 (e) 962
4 (a) 500 (b) 420 (c) 239 (d) 303 (e) 364
5 (a) 2723 (b) 3837 (c) 9717

6 109	**7** 61	**8** 122	**9** 91
10 115	**11** 120	**12** 121	**13** 144
14 788	**15** 411	**16** 610	**17** 1310
18 1420	**19** 8100	**20** 13 000	**21** 27
22 38	**23** 25	**24** 35	**25** 58
26 180	**27** 170	**28** 260	**29** 363
30 171	**31** 377	**32** 826	**33** 1600
34 7355	**35** 3327		

HOMEWORK

Page 3

HOMEWORK ANSWERS

Page 133

Mental strategies for addition and subtraction

 **Do not use a calculator**

1 Write down the first ten numbers obtained if 25 keeps being added to 62.

2 Write down the first ten numbers obtained if 19 keeps being subtracted from 453.

3 What needs to be added to each of these numbers to make 1000?
    (a) 400   **(b)** 670   **(c)** 355   **(d)** 505   **(e)** 38

4 What needs to be added to each of these numbers to make 650?
    (a) 150   **(b)** 230   **(c)** 411   **(d)** 347   **(e)** 286

5 Given that $356 + 468 + 589 + 623 + 714 + 967 = 3717$, write down the answers to these without using any working.
    (a) $357 + 469 + 590 + 624 + 715 + 968$
    (b) $376 + 488 + 609 + 643 + 734 + 987$
    (c) $1356 + 1468 + 1589 + 1623 + 1714 + 1967$

Calculate each of these.

6 $83 + 26$ **7** $37 + 24$ **8** $33 + 89$ **9** $47 + 44$

10 $58 + 57$ **11** $54 + 66$ **12** $33 + 88$ **13** $86 + 58$

14 $26 + 762$ **15** $357 + 54$ **16** $180 + 430$ **17** $530 + 780$

18 $690 + 730$ **19** $5700 + 2400$ **20** $7100 + 5900$ **21** $57 - 30$

22 $55 - 17$ **23** $54 - 29$ **24** $72 - 37$ **25** $83 - 25$

26 $540 - 360$ **27** $840 - 670$ **28** $440 - 180$ **29** $633 - 270$

30 $720 - 549$ **31** $476 - 99$ **32** $850 - 24$ **33** $5100 - 3500$

34 $8354 - 999$ **35** $6727 - 3400$

1 Mental strategies for addition and subtraction

 **Do not use a calculator**

Only answers are needed.

1 Write down the first ten numbers obtained if 15 keeps being added to 38.

2 Write down the first ten numbers obtained if 7 keeps being subtracted from 2000.

3 Write down the first ten numbers obtained if 39 keeps being subtracted from 5000.

4 What needs to be added to each of these numbers to make 100?
   (a) 60   **(b)** 85   **(c)** 42   **(d)** 67   **(e)** 3

5 What needs to be added to each of these numbers to make 2000?
   (a) 700   **(b)** 340   **(c)** 465   **(d)** 687   **(e)** 1018

6 What needs to be added to each of these numbers to make 350?
   (a) 140   **(b)** 280   **(c)** 128   **(d)** 78   **(e)** 312

7 Given that $567 + 393 + 836 + 441 + 1729 = 3966$, write down the answers to these without using any working.
   (a) $566 + 392 + 835 + 440 + 1728$ **(b)** $5670 + 3930 + 8360 + 4410 + 17\ 290$
   (c) $2567 + 2393 + 2836 + 2441 + 3729$

8 Find the numbers to go in the squares.
   (a) $8 + 15 = 11 + \square$ **(b)** $83 + 28 = \square + 38$
   (c) $436 + 187 = 236 + \square$ **(d)** $47 - 18 = 60 - \square$
   (e) $432 - \square = 632 - 263$ **(f)** $\square - 539 = 3478 + 1639$

Calculate each of these.

9 $58 + 38$ **10** $64 + 77$ **11** $16 + 67$ **12** $59 + 62$

13 $85 + 37$ **14** $19 + 96$ **15** $67 + 75$ **16** $136 + 73$

17 $647 + 39$ **18** $847 + 76$ **19** $470 + 770$ **20** $960 + 580$

21 $4600 + 190$ **22** $4800 + 3500$ **23** $5300 + 3800$ **24** $67 - 23$

25 $98 - 39$ **26** $75 - 47$ **27** $83 - 66$ **28** $75 - 37$

29 $520 - 170$ **30** $660 - 470$ **31** $353 - 140$ **32** $835 - 250$

33 $925 - 650$ **34** $653 - 27$ **35** $6700 - 4500$ **36** $5700 - 2800$

2

Multiplying and dividing mentally by single digits and powers of 10

LESSON OBJECTIVES

- Recall all multiplication facts up to 10 × 10 and use them to derive quickly the corresponding division facts
- Understand and use unit fractions as multiplicative inverses
- Multiply or divide integers by powers of 10
- Develop a range of strategies for mental calculation

WORKING INTERACTIVELY

- Check that all multiplication facts up to 9 × 9 can be done automatically.
- Check that students are clear that all of these statements are equivalent and can be deduced from 9 × 4 = 36:

36 divided by 9 is 4	36 divided by 4 is 9
$36 \div 9 = 4$	$36 \div 4 = 9$
$\dfrac{36}{9} = 4$	$\dfrac{36}{4} = 9$
one ninth $\left(\dfrac{1}{9}\right)$ of 36 is 4	one quarter $\left(\dfrac{1}{4}\right)$ of 36 is 9
$\dfrac{1}{9} \times 36 = 4$	$\dfrac{1}{4} \times 36 = 9$
$36 \times \dfrac{1}{9} = 4$	$36 \times \dfrac{1}{4} = 9$
9 into 36 goes 4 times	4 into 36 goes 9 times
$9)\overline{36}^{\,4}$	$4)\overline{36}^{\,9}$

- Discuss strategies for working out calculations like 300 × 20 = 6000 (e.g. 3 × 2 = 6, 100 × 10 = 1000).
- Point out that care is needed with some products, such as 80 × 50 = 4000, because of the extra zero (e.g. 8 × 5 = 40, 10 × 10 = 100).
- Discuss strategies for carrying out calculations like 600 ÷ 30 = 20 (600 ÷ 30 = 60 ÷ 3 = 20).

It is suggested that you avoid decimals. These are covered in lessons 17 and 18.

INDIVIDUAL WORK

Students work through the classwork sheet.

Review

Mark classwork and review strategies. In particular, ensure students appreciate that dividing by 4, for example, is equivalent to multiplying by $\dfrac{1}{4}$, and know how to multiply and divide numbers by powers of 10.

ANSWERS TO THE CLASSWORK SHEET

1 (a) 12 (b) 120 (c) 1200 (d) 1200

2 (a) 35 (b) 350 (c) 3500 (d) 3500

3 (a) 360 (b) 60 (c) 150 (d) 400 (e) 3000
(f) 8100 (g) 560 000 (h) 100 000

4 (a) 4 (b) 13 (c) 13 (d) 346 (e) 50 (f) 66
(g) 8 (h) 20

5 (a) 4 (b) 60 (c) 400 (d) 60

6 (a) 8 (b) 70 (c) 7 (d) 7

7 (a) 60 (b) 300 (c) 70 (d) 4 (e) 500 (f) 80
(g) 50 (h) 5

8 (a) 150 (b) 6 (c) 60 (d) 21 000 (e) 200 000
(f) 80 (g) 3600 (h) 1 000 000

HOMEWORK

Page
6

HOMEWORK
ANSWERS
Page
133

Lessons in Numeracy (Intermediate) © Longman (an imprint of **PEARSON** Education) 2001

2

Multiplying and dividing mentally by single digits and powers of 10

Do not use a calculator

Calculate these.

1 (a) 3×4 (b) 30×4 (c) 30×40 (d) 3×400

2 (a) 5×7 (b) 7×50 (c) 7×500 (d) 50×70

3 (a) 9×40 (b) 20×3 (c) 3×50 (d) 20×20

     (e) 50×60 (f) 9×900 (g) 700×800 (h) 500×200

4 (a) $400 \div 100$ (b) $1300 \div 100$ (c) $\dfrac{1300}{100}$ (d) $\dfrac{1}{10} \times 3460$

     (e) $5000 \times \dfrac{1}{100}$ (f) $\dfrac{1}{100} \times 6600$ (g) $\dfrac{8000}{1000}$ (h) $20\,000 \div 1000$

5 (a) $24 \div 6$ (b) $240 \div 4$ (c) $\dfrac{1}{6} \times 2400$ (d) $2400 \times \dfrac{1}{40}$

6 (a) $56 \div 7$ (b) $\dfrac{560}{8}$ (c) $\dfrac{1}{80} \times 560$ (d) $5600 \div 800$

7 (a) $\dfrac{1}{5} \times 300$ (b) $\dfrac{900}{3}$ (c) $350 \div 5$ (d) $\dfrac{1}{60} \times 240$

     (e) $4000 \times \dfrac{1}{8}$ (f) $560 \div 7$ (g) $\dfrac{4500}{90}$ (h) $1000 \times \dfrac{1}{200}$

8 (a) 5×30 (b) $\dfrac{1}{5} \times 30$ (c) $480 \times \dfrac{1}{8}$ (d) 300×70

     (e) 4000×50 (f) $\dfrac{1}{50} \times 4000$ (g) 60^2 (h) 5000×200

2 Multiplying and dividing mentally by single digits and powers of 10

 **Do not use a calculator**

Calculate these.

1 (a) 4×5 (b) 50×4 (c) 40×50 (d) 5×400

2 (a) 6×8 (b) 6×80 (c) 8×600 (d) 800×60

3 (a) 7×50 (b) 40×4 (c) 4×60 (d) 80×80

   (e) 30×70 (f) 700×7 (g) 600×600 (h) 500×600

4 (a) $800 \div 100$ (b) $2700 \div 100$ (c) $\frac{4500}{10}$ (d) $5380 \times \frac{1}{10}$

   (e) $13\,000 \times \frac{1}{1000}$ (f) $\frac{1}{100} \times 13\,800$ (g) $\frac{5000}{500}$ (h) $4000 \div 100$

5 (a) $\frac{18}{3}$ (b) $180 \div 30$ (c) $\frac{1}{60} \times 18\,000$ (d) $1800 \times \frac{1}{600}$

6 (a) $63 \div 9$ (b) $\frac{1}{7} \times 630$ (c) $630 \times \frac{1}{90}$ (d) $\frac{6300}{7}$

7 (a) $\frac{1}{8} \times 400$ (b) $\frac{300}{6}$ (c) $450 \div 5$ (d) $420 \times \frac{1}{7}$

   (e) $8100 \div 90$ (f) $2700 \times \frac{1}{9}$ (g) $3600 \div 400$ (h) $4000 \times \frac{1}{8}$

8 (a) 70×70 (b) $2500 \times \frac{1}{5}$ (c) 6000×8 (d) $1800 \times \frac{1}{30}$

   (e) 200×500 (f) $6000 \times \frac{1}{6000}$ (g) 80×40 (h) $\frac{1}{40} \times 8000$

   (i) 70^2 (j) $\frac{1}{300} \times 24\,000$

Lessons in Numeracy (Intermediate) © Longman (an imprint of Pearson Education) 2001

3 Multiplying whole numbers

> **LESSON OBJECTIVES**
>
> ● Use standard column procedures for multiplication of integers of any size
> ● Use and compare alternative strategies for multiplication of integers of any size

WORKING INTERACTIVELY

● Check students are confident about questions like these (the procedures in brackets are some alternatives to the standard algorithm):

71×6	(e.g. $70 \times 6 + 6 = 420 + 6 = 426$)
79×8	(e.g. $80 \times 8 - 8 = 640 - 8 = 632$)
190×7	(e.g. $200 \times 7 - 10 \times 7 = 1400 - 70 = 1330$)
440×9	(e.g. $400 \times 9 + 40 \times 9 = 3600 + 360 = 3960$)

● How do students work out 23×57? ($= 1311$)

There are various alternatives to the standard algorithm.

Method 1 23×57

	50	7
20	1000	140
3	150	21

$$1000 + 140 + 150 + 21 = 1311$$

Method 2 23×57

3×57	$=\ \ 171$
20×57	$= \underline{1140}$
23×57	$= 1311$

Method 3 (Gelosia)

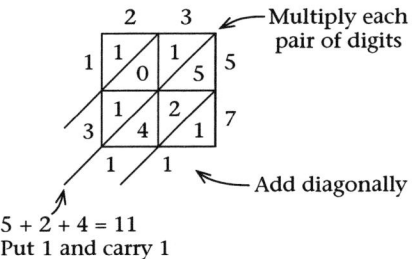

Multiply each pair of digits

Add diagonally

$5 + 2 + 4 = 11$
Put 1 and carry 1

● Try other 2-digit × 2-digit examples.
● What about 123×36? ($= 4428$)
● Try other 3-digit × 2-digit examples.

INDIVIDUAL WORK

Put more questions of the same type on the board for students to do.

You could set questions involving more than 3 digits × 2 digits. Students could make up examples for each other to do.

Review

Mark any classwork and review strategies. This can include further discussion of the standard algorithm, compared with the alternatives.

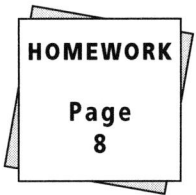

HOMEWORK

Page
8

HOMEWORK
ANSWERS
Page
133

3 Multiplying whole numbers

Do not use a calculator

Calculate these.

1. 37 × 21
2. 63 × 19
3. 26 × 33
4. 36 × 24
5. 53 × 27
6. 48 × 39
7. 57 × 68
8. 89 × 77
9. 23 × 75
10. 74 × 28
11. 180 × 46
12. 132 × 18
13. 472 × 38
14. 509 × 47
15. 835 × 72
16. 693 × 66
17. 1038 × 57
18. 3509 × 37
19. 4382 × 76
20. 833 × 143

Lessons in Numeracy (Intermediate) © Longman (an imprint of Pearson Education) 2001

8

INTERMEDIATE ● HOMEWORK

3 Multiplying whole numbers

Do not use a calculator

Calculate these.

1. 37 × 21
2. 63 × 19
3. 26 × 33
4. 36 × 24
5. 53 × 27
6. 48 × 39
7. 57 × 68
8. 89 × 77
9. 23 × 75
10. 74 × 28
11. 180 × 46
12. 132 × 18
13. 472 × 38
14. 509 × 47
15. 835 × 72
16. 693 × 66
17. 1038 × 57
18. 3509 × 37
19. 4382 × 76
20. 833 × 143

Lessons in Numeracy (Intermediate) © Longman (an imprint of Pearson Education) 2001

4 Dividing whole numbers

LESSON OBJECTIVES

● Understand and use an efficient method for dividing by integers of any size
● Use different ways of expressing the answer, where the division is inexact
● Develop a range of strategies for mental calculation

WORKING INTERACTIVELY

● Check students are confident about questions like these:

366 ÷ 6	(= 61)
128 ÷ 8	(= 16)
434 ÷ 7	(= 62)
477 ÷ 9	(= 53)

● How do students work out 2055 ÷ 15? (= 137)

● What about divisions that lead to a remainder, such as 94 ÷ 7? Sometimes leaving the answer in the form 13 r 3 is sensible (e.g. 94 days is 13 weeks 3 days). In other cases, either a **mixed number** answer $\left(94 \div 7 = 13\frac{3}{7}\right)$ or a decimal answer (94 ÷ 7 is about 13.4) may be appropriate.

> Work on rounding numbers to a given number of decimal places or significant figures is in lesson 25 and short division to turn a fraction into a decimal is in lesson 15.

● What about 4879 ÷ 38? (= 128, remainder 15)

Here is one alternative to the standard algorithm.

$$
\begin{array}{rr}
 & 4879 \\
100 \times 38 & -3800 \\
\hline
 & 1079 \\
20 \times 38 & -760 \\
\hline
 & 319 \\
5 \times 38 & -190 \\
\hline
 & 129 \\
3 \times 38 & -114 \\
\hline
 & \mathbf{15}
\end{array}
$$

So the answer is (100 + 20 + 5 + 3) r 15 = 128 r 15
The algorithm can be continued, to express the answer as a decimal.

$$
\begin{array}{rr}
 & 15 \\
0.3 \times 38 & -11.4 \\
\hline
 & 3.6 \\
0.05 \times 38 & -1.9 \\
\hline
 & 1.7
\end{array}
$$

So the answer is 128.4, correct to 1 decimal place.

● Point out that division by large numbers can often be made simpler:
360 ÷ 90 = 36 ÷ 9 = 4
480 ÷ 15 = 960 ÷ 30 = 96 ÷ 3 = 32
1356 ÷ 36 = 678 ÷ 18 = 339 ÷ 9 = 113 ÷ 3 = $37\frac{2}{3}$ = 37.7 (to 1 decimal place)
9400 ÷ 70 = 940 ÷ 7 = $134\frac{2}{7}$ = 134.3 (to 1 decimal place)

INDIVIDUAL WORK

Students work through the classwork sheet.

Review

Mark any classwork and review strategies and, in particular, the standard algorithm for division.

ANSWERS TO THE CLASSWORK SHEET

1 52		**2** 78		**3** 47		**4** 42	
5 57		**6** 26		**7** 485		**8** 336	
9 59		**10** 71		**11** 47		**12** 56	

13 16 r 1 or $16\frac{1}{3}$ or 16.3   **14** 8 r 4 or $8\frac{4}{7}$ or 8.6
15 6 r 2 or $6\frac{2}{13}$ or 6.2   **16** 5 r 5 or $5\frac{5}{49}$ or 5.1

HOMEWORK

Page 11

HOMEWORK ANSWERS Page 133

4 Dividing whole numbers

Do not use a calculator

Calculate these. Use any method you like, including making the division simpler.

1 156 ÷ 3   **2** 390 ÷ 5   **3** 329 ÷ 7

4 504 ÷ 12   **5** 855 ÷ 15   **6** 468 ÷ 18

7 8245 ÷ 17   **8** 8736 ÷ 26   **9** 3717 ÷ 63

10 5041 ÷ 71   **11** 9870 ÷ 210   **12** 4648 ÷ 83

Calculate these. The answers are not exact. Give each answer in three forms: with a remainder *and* as a mixed number *and* correct to 1 decimal place.

13 49 ÷ 3   **14** 60 ÷ 7   **15** 80 ÷ 13

16 250 ÷ 49

Lessons in Numeracy (Intermediate) © Longman (an imprint of Pearson Education) 2001

10

INTERMEDIATE ● CLASSWORK

4 Dividing whole numbers

Do not use a calculator

Calculate these. Use any method you like, including making the division simpler.

1 156 ÷ 3   **2** 390 ÷ 5   **3** 329 ÷ 7

4 504 ÷ 12   **5** 855 ÷ 15   **6** 468 ÷ 18

7 8245 ÷ 17   **8** 8736 ÷ 26   **9** 3717 ÷ 63

10 5041 ÷ 71   **11** 9870 ÷ 210   **12** 4648 ÷ 83

Calculate these. The answers are not exact. Give each answer in three forms: with a remainder *and* as a mixed number *and* correct to 1 decimal place.

13 49 ÷ 3   **14** 60 ÷ 7   **15** 80 ÷ 13

16 250 ÷ 49

Lessons in Numeracy (Intermediate) © Longman (an imprint of Pearson Education) 2001

4 Dividing whole numbers

Do not use a calculator

Calculate these. Use any method you like, including making the division simpler.

1 232 ÷ 4 **2** 135 ÷ 5 **3** 343 ÷ 7

4 612 ÷ 9 **5** 312 ÷ 12 **6** 875 ÷ 25

7 576 ÷ 24 **8** 416 ÷ 13 **9** 494 ÷ 19

10 1462 ÷ 34 **11** 4836 ÷ 62 **12** 4257 ÷ 99

Calculate these. The answers are not exact. Give each answer in three forms: with a remainder *and* as a mixed number *and* correct to 1 decimal place.

13 29 ÷ 3 **14** 53 ÷ 5 **15** 69 ÷ 7

16 100 ÷ 12 **17** 90 ÷ 17 **18** 200 ÷ 23

19 423 ÷ 39 **20** 2569 ÷ 71

Lessons in Numeracy (Intermediate) © Longman (an imprint of Pearson Education) 2001

INTERMEDIATE ● HOMEWORK

4 Dividing whole numbers

Do not use a calculator

Calculate these. Use any method you like, including making the division simpler.

1 232 ÷ 4 **2** 135 ÷ 5 **3** 343 ÷ 7

4 612 ÷ 9 **5** 312 ÷ 12 **6** 875 ÷ 25

7 576 ÷ 24 **8** 416 ÷ 13 **9** 494 ÷ 19

10 1462 ÷ 34 **11** 4836 ÷ 62 **12** 4257 ÷ 99

Calculate these. The answers are not exact. Give each answer in three forms: with a remainder *and* as a mixed number *and* correct to 1 decimal place.

13 29 ÷ 3 **14** 53 ÷ 5 **15** 69 ÷ 7

16 100 ÷ 12 **17** 90 ÷ 17 **18** 200 ÷ 23

19 423 ÷ 39 **20** 2569 ÷ 71

Lessons in Numeracy (Intermediate) © Longman (an imprint of Pearson Education) 2001

5 Selecting the correct operation to solve problems

LESSON OBJECTIVES

● Draw on knowledge of operations, inverse operations and place value to select and use suitable strategies and techniques to solve problems

● Use efficient methods to multiply and divide numbers

● Develop a range of strategies for mental calculation

WORKING INTERACTIVELY

● Check students are confident about questions like these, especially choosing which operation needs to be done:

Ice creams cost 65p each.
How much do 10 cost? (£6.50)

Ice creams cost 65p each.
How many can you buy for £10?
(15 and 25p change)

Coaches seat 49 passengers.
How many are needed for a party of 260?
(6 coaches and 34 empty seats)

80 packets of pins each contain 47 pins.
How many pins altogether? (3760)

80 packets of pins cost £16.
How much does each packet cost? (20p)

INDIVIDUAL WORK

Do questions 1 to 6 of the classwork sheet.

WORKING INTERACTIVELY

● You are given the digits 3, 5 and 7. Discuss with students how to replace the three stars in each of these with these three digits in some order, so as to get an answer that is (a) as large as possible, (b) as small as possible, but still positive.

$** + *$ ((a) $75 + 3 = 78$ or $73 + 5 = 78$)
　　　　((b) $35 + 7 = 42$ or $37 + 5 = 42$)

$** - *$ ((a) $75 - 3 = 72$)　　(b) $35 - 7 = 28$)

$** \times *$ ((a) $73 \times 5 = 365$)　　(b) $37 \times 5 = 185$)

$* + * - *$ ((a) $7 + 5 - 3 = 9$ or $5 + 7 - 3 = 9$)
　　　　((b) $3 + 5 - 7 = 1$ or $5 + 3 - 7 = 1$)

$* \times * - *$ ((a) $7 \times 5 - 3 = 32$ or $5 \times 7 - 3 = 32$)
　　　　((b) $3 \times 5 - 7 = 8$ or $5 \times 3 - 7 = 8$)

$* \times * + *$ ((a) $7 \times 5 + 3 = 38$ or $5 \times 7 + 3 = 38$)
　　　　((b) $3 \times 5 + 7 = 22$ or $5 \times 3 + 7 = 22$)

INDIVIDUAL WORK

Do questions 7 and 8 of the classwork sheet.

Review

Mark any classwork and discuss the strategy needed to solve each problem.

ANSWERS TO THE CLASSWORK SHEET

1　17 coaches

2　1051 people

3　(a) 15 pies　(b) 25p

4　42 mousses

5　142 bags

6　(a) 102 960 escudos　(b) £13

7　(a) (i) 16 (subtract the 5)　(ii) 10 (subtract the 8)
　　(b) (i) 161 (e.g. $86 + 75$)　(ii) 125 (e.g. $57 + 68$)
　　(c) (i) 31 ($87 - 56$)　(ii) 7 ($75 - 68$)
　　(d) (i) 881 (e.g. $876 + 5$)　(ii) 575 (e.g. $567 + 8$)
　　(e) (i) 603 ($76 \times 8 - 5$)　(ii) 327 ($67 \times 5 - 8$)

8　(a) $28 + 59 = 87$　　　　(b) $52 + 8 + 9 = 69$
　　(c) $82 + 5 - 9 = 78$　　　(d) $8 \times 9 + 5 + 2 = 79$
　　(e) $2 \times 5 + 8 \times 9 = 82$　(f) $58 \times 2 - 9 = 107$

```
HOMEWORK

Page
14
```

```
HOMEWORK
ANSWERS
Page
133
```

5

Selecting the correct operation to solve problems

Do not use a calculator for questions 1 to 6

1 The police want to transport 450 men using police coaches. Each police coach holds a maximum of 27 men. How many coaches are needed?

2 A bus company is providing 16 buses for a pop concert.
Each bus can carry a maximum of 69 passengers.
The total number of empty seats is 53.
How many people are the buses taking to the concert?

3 Someone has £5.50 to spend on pork pies for a party.
(a) Each pork pie costs 35p. How many pies are bought?
(b) How much money is left over?

4 A caterer buys milk in 3 litre containers. Each mousse being made for a party contains 70 ml of milk. How many mousses can be made using one container of milk?

5 A trader buys 10 kg of a spice and puts it into 70 g bags to sell. How many bags can be filled?

6 A man travelling to Portugal received 312 escudos for each £1.
(a) He changed £330 into escudos. How much did he receive in escudos?
(b) He paid 4056 escudos for a meal. How much is this in pounds?

You may use a calculator for questions 7 and 8

7 You are given the digits 5, 6, 7 and 8. Replace the four stars in each of these with these four digits in some order, so as to get an answer that is
(i) as large as possible
(ii) as small as possible, but bigger than zero.

(a) $* + * + * - *$ (b) $** + **$ (c) $** - **$ (d) $*** + *$ (e) $** \times * - *$

8 You are given the four digits 2, 5, 8 and 9. Replace the four stars in each of these with these four digits in some order, so as to get an answer that is as close to 80 as possible. (Sometimes it is not possible to get very close.)

(a) $** + **$ (b) $** + * + *$ (c) $** + * - *$ (d) $* \times * + * + *$
(e) $* \times * + * \times *$ (f) $** \times * - *$

 5 Selecting the correct operation to solve problems

 Do not use a calculator for questions 1 to 8

1 The cost of tickets for a pop concert is £33 per person. What is the total cost for a party of 26 people?

2 Wayne saves £3.50 each week for a present for his mum. The present costs £30. How many weeks will he need to save for it?

3 In a magazine there are 48 pages. The average number of words on each page is 750. About how many words are there in the magazine?

4 Each bag of sweets contains 27 sweets. How many bags need to be bought to obtain 500 sweets?

5 A man buys 13 notebooks for a special project. He gets 58p change from a five pound note. How much is each notebook?

6 John pays £75 deposit for a computer and then monthly instalments of £34.50 for two years. What is the total amount he pays for the computer?

7 The same shirt is on sale in England and France. In England it costs £25 and it costs 295 francs in France. The exchange rate is 11 francs for each £1. In which country is the shirt cheaper? Explain your answer.

8 13 identical cylindrical storage jars are placed next to each other on a shelf 1.48 m long and there is then just enough room for a recipe book 5 cm thick. What is the diameter of each jar?

You may use a calculator for questions 9 and 10

9 You are given the digits 4, 5 and 6. Replace the three stars in each of these with these three digits in some order, so as to get an answer that is
  (i) as large as possible
  (ii) as small as possible, but bigger than zero.

  (a) $* + * - *$
  (b) $** + *$
  (c) $** - *$
  (d) $** \times *$
  (e) $* \times * - *$
  (f) $* \times * + *$

10 You are given the six digits 3, 4, 5, 6, 7 and 8. Replace the six stars in each of these with these six digits in some order, so as to get the answers given.
  (a) $** + ** + ** = 159$
  (b) $** + * + * - * - * = 30$
  (c) $*** \times * + * - * = 1367$
  (d) $* \times * + * \times * + * \times * = 83$
  (e) $** - ** + * - * = 54$
  (f) $* \times * + * \times * - * - * = 36$

6 Negative numbers 1

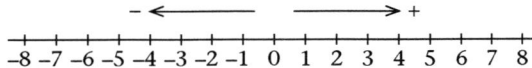

LESSON OBJECTIVES

● Understand and use negative integers, both as positions and translations on a number line

● Add and subtract negative numbers

WORKING INTERACTIVELY

Note on vocabulary:
If –4 is called **negative** 4 then expressions such 3 – (–4) can be read as '3 minus negative 4'.

● Put this number line on the board.

$$\overset{-\ \longleftarrow\ \longrightarrow\ +}{\underset{-8\ -7\ -6\ -5\ -4\ -3\ -2\ -1\ \ 0\ \ 1\ \ 2\ \ 3\ \ 4\ \ 5\ \ 6\ \ 7\ \ 8}{\mid\ \mid\ \mid\ \mid\ \mid\ \mid\ \mid\ \mid\ \mid\ \mid\ \mid\ \mid\ \mid\ \mid\ \mid\ \mid\ \mid}}$$

● Which is greater:
–5 or 3?   –2 or –6?
–19 or –21?   19 or 21?

● Invite students round the class to answer questions 1 and 2 from the classwork sheet (or this could be done individually).

● Adding can be thought of as a **translation** on the number line. Adding a positive number is a translation to the right: adding a negative number is a translation to the left.

So,

$-3 + 5 = 2$ (start at –3 on the number line and move 5 to the right)
$-8 + 2 = -6$
$-3 + 3 = 0$
$2 + 3 = 5$
$-4 + (-3) = -7$ (start at –4 and move 3 to the left)
$2 + (-5) = -3$
$4 + (-4) = 0$
$8 + (-5) = 3$

● Subtracting can be thought of as 'difference': what you add to the second number to get the first.

So,

$7 - 3 = 4$ (to get from 3 to 7, move 4 *to the right*)
$3 - (-4) = 7$ (to get from –4 to 3, move 7 *to the right*)
$-2 - 3 = -5$ (to get from 3 to –2, move 5 *to the left*)
$-4 - (-7) = 3$ (to get from –7 to –4, move 3 *to the right*)
$-5 - (-1) = -4$ (to get from –1 to –5, move 4 *to the left*)

● Alternatively, subtraction can be thought of as the **inverse** operation to addition. This means that 'subtract 3' is the same as 'add negative 3' and 'subtract negative 4' is the same as 'add 4'.

So, $7 - 3 = 7 + (-3) = 4$
$3 - (-4) = 3 + 4 = 7$
$-2 - 3 = -2 + (-3) = -5$
$-4 - (-7) = -4 + 7 = 3$
$-5 - (-1) = -5 + 1 = -4$

INDIVIDUAL WORK

Students work through the classwork sheet.

Review

Mark any classwork and review strategies:
● Adding a positive number (+ +) and subtracting a negative number (– –) have the same effect.
● Subtracting a positive number (– +) and adding a negative number (+ –) have the same effect.

ANSWERS TO THE CLASSWORK SHEET

1 (a) 3 (b) –8 (c) –7 (d) –5 (e) –3 (f) –10
2 (a) 4 (b) –6 (c) 2 (d) 11 (e) 5 (f) 0
3 (a) 13 (b) 3 (c) –3 (d) 0 (e) 2 (f) –4
(g) –13 (h) 0 (i) –4 (j) –7 (k) 4 (l) –18
(m) 8 (n) 12 (o) 2 (p) –3 (q) –5 (r) –7
(s) 4 (t) –8 (u) 0
4 (a) –13 (b) 5 (c) –28 (d) –13 (e) –18 (f) 13
(g) 8 (h) 31 (i) –31 (j) –25 (k) 40 (l) 8
(m) –15 (n) 115 (o) –15 (p) 15 (q) –9 (r) –1
(s) 1 (t) –1 (u) 7

HOMEWORK

Page 17

HOMEWORK ANSWERS Page 133

6 Negative numbers 1

 **Do not use a calculator**

1 Which number in each pair is less?

(a) 8, 3   (b) −8, 3   (c) −4, −7

(d) 0, −5   (e) −3, 6   (f) 20, −10

2 Which number in each set is greatest?

(a) 4, −5, 3   (b) −6, −8, −11   (c) 0, 2, −2

(d) 5, 11, 2   (e) 1, −10, 5   (f) 0, −7, −3

Calculate these.

3 (a) 5 + 8   (b) −5 + 8   (c) −6 + 3   (d) −4 + 4

(e) 7 + (−5)   (f) 3 + (−7)   (g) −4 + (−9)   (h) 3 + (−3)

(i) 4 − 8   (j) −3 − 4   (k) 11 − 7   (l) −7 − 11

(m) 6 − (−2)   (n) 4 − (−8)   (o) −3 − (−5)   (p) −4 − (−1)

(q) 0 + (−5)   (r) 0 − 7   (s) 0 − (−4)   (t) −8 − 0

(u) −5 − (−5)

4 (a) 4 − 17   (b) 14 + (−9)   (c) −23 − 5

(d) −16 − (−3)   (e) −13 + (−5)   (f) 0 − (−13)

(g) 26 − 18   (h) 23 − (−8)   (i) −16 + (−15)

(j) −43 + 18   (k) 28 − (−12)   (l) −17 − (−25)

(m) 50 − 65   (n) 65 − (−50)   (o) −65 + 50

(p) −50 − (−65)   (q) 3 − 5 − 7   (r) −5 + 6 + (−2)

(s) 4 − (−5) − 8   (t) 13 − 17 − 15 − (−18)   (u) 7 − (−7) + (−7)

Lessons in Numeracy (Intermediate) © Longman (an imprint of Pearson Education) 2001

6 Negative numbers 1

Do not use a calculator

1 Which number in each pair is less?

(a) 7, −4   (b) −9, 5   (c) −6, −9   (d) −17, 0

2 Which number in each set is greatest?

(a) −6, −8, 4   (b) −3, −5, −7

(c) 6, 9, −12   (d) 5, −10, 15, −20

Calculate these.

3 (a) −3 + 9   (b) 3 + 9   (c) −8 + 6   (d) −7 + 7

(e) 4 + (−6)   (f) 8 + (−7)   (g) −6 + (−7)   (h) 5 + (−10)

(i) −7 − 3   (j) 5 − 9   (k) 13 − 12   (l) −8 − 8

(m) 5 − (−10)   (n) 11 − (−3)

4 (a) 5 + (−16)   (b) 13 − 19   (c) −16 − 17

(d) −15 − (−8)   (e) 23 − (−24)   (f) −18 + (−13)

(g) 37 − 37   (h) 25 − (−50)   (i) 0 + (−17)

(j) −46 + 52   (k) 0 − (−13)   (l) −28 − 0

(m) −38 + 22   (n) −42 + (−16)   (o) −29 − (−29)

(p) 43 − 43

5 (a) −3 + 4 − 7 − (−2)   (b) 16 − 18 + (−20) − (−22) + 24

Lessons in Numeracy (Intermediate) © Longman (an imprint of Pearson Education) 2001

7 Negative numbers 2

LESSON OBJECTIVES
● Multiply and divide negative numbers

WORKING INTERACTIVELY

Put this multiplication table on the board and ask students to complete it by paying attention to the sequences in each row and column.

×	−4	−3	−2	−1	0	1	2	3	4
−4									
−3									
−2									
−1									
0					0	0	0	0	0
1					0	1	2	3	4
2					0	2	4	6	8
3					0	3	6	9	12
4					0	4	8	12	16

● The patterns in the completed table can then be discussed.

×	−4	−3	−2	−1	0	1	2	3	4
−4	16	12	8	4	0	−4	−8	−12	−16
−3	12	9	6	3	0	−3	−6	−9	−12
−2	8	6	4	2	0	−2	−4	−6	−8
−1	4	3	2	1	0	−1	−2	−3	−4
0	0	0	0	0	0	0	0	0	0
1	−4	−3	−2	−1	0	1	2	3	4
2	−8	−6	−4	−2	0	2	4	6	8
3	−12	−9	−6	−3	0	3	6	9	12
4	−16	−12	−8	−4	0	4	8	12	16

● Students can observe that:
   positive × positive is positive
   negative × negative is positive
   positive × negative is negative
   negative × positive is negative
and note that this is equivalent to the results discussed in the review for lesson 6.

● Discuss how the table can be used backwards to deduce results such as:
$$9 \div (-3) = -3$$
$$(-8) \div 4 = -2$$
$$(-12) \div (-4) = 3$$
Thus the 'sign rules' for dividing negative numbers are the same as those for multiplying negative numbers.

INDIVIDUAL WORK

Students work through the classwork sheet. This includes some questions that revisit addition and subtraction of negative numbers.

Review

Mark any classwork and summarise the strategies for all four operations:

● Remember, for both multiplication and division:
   if one sign is negative, the answer is negative
   if both signs are negative, the answer is positive.

● Adding a positive number (+ +) and subtracting a negative number (− −) have the same effect.

● Subtracting a positive number (− +) and adding a negative number (+ −) have the same effect.

ANSWERS TO THE CLASSWORK SHEET

1 (a) −8 (b) 15 (c) −48 (d) 63 (e) 20 (f) 9
   (g) 0 (h) −36 (i) 14 (j) 0 (k) 17 (l) −8
2 (a) 3 (b) −4 (c) 7 (d) −3 (e) −1 (f) −10
   (g) 4 (h) 9 (i) −2 (j) 0 (k) −2 (l) 7
3 (a) −20 (b) −4 (c) −12 (d) 25 (e) 4 (f) 63
   (g) −4 (h) 8 (i) −8 (j) −1 (k) 1 (l) −24
4 (a) 8 (b) 16 (c) −48 (d) −3 (e) −3 (f) 2
   (g) −2 (h) −4 (i) 9 (j) 17 (k) 10 (l) 0

HOMEWORK	HOMEWORK ANSWERS
Page 20	Page 133

7 Negative numbers 2

Do not use a calculator

1 Calculate these multiplications.

(a) 2×-4　　(b) -5×-3　　(c) -8×6　　(d) 7×9

(e) -5×-4　　(f) $(-3)^2$　　(g) -5×0　　(h) -4×9

(i) -7×-2　　(j) 0×9　　(k) -17×-1　　(l) $(-2)^3$

2 Calculate these divisions.

(a) $-6 \div -2$　　(b) $12 \div -3$　　(c) $49 \div 7$　　(d) $-24 \div 8$

(e) $6 \div -6$　　(f) $-30 \div 3$　　(g) $-20 \div -5$　　(h) $-36 \div -4$

(i) $18 \div -9$　　(j) $0 \div -6$　　(k) $-28 \div 14$　　(l) $-56 \div -8$

3 Calculate these.

(a) -4×5　　(b) $1/2 \times -8$　　(c) $-12 \div 1$　　(d) $(-5)^2$

(e) $-16 \div -4$　　(f) -9×-7　　(g) $-12 \times \frac{1}{3}$　　(h) $\frac{-48}{-6}$

(i) $\frac{8}{-1}$　　(j) $\frac{1}{5} \times -5$　　(k) $(-1)^4$　　(l) $-2 \times -3 \times -4$

4 Calculate these.

(a) $12 + (-4)$　　(b) $12 - (-4)$　　(c) 12×-4　　(d) $12 \div -4$

(e) $-6 - (-3)$　　(f) $-6 \div -3$　　(g) $\frac{8 - 12}{2}$　　(h) $\frac{-4 - 16}{5}$

(i) $\frac{-5 + (-4)}{-5 - (-4)}$　　(j) $-3 \times -4 - (-5)$　　(k) $6 - \frac{8}{-2}$　　(l) $\frac{-10}{-5} + \frac{12}{-6}$

7 Negative numbers 2

Do not use a calculator

1 Calculate these multiplications.

(a) -6×-4 (b) -7×5 (c) 3×-6 (d) -4×-8

(e) $(-6)^2$ (f) 4×7 (g) 0×5 (h) -7×0

(i) -3×8 (j) -7×-4 (k) $(-3)^2$ (l) -1×-11

2 Calculate these divisions.

(a) $16 \div -4$ (b) $36 \div 6$ (c) $-8 \div -2$ (d) $5 \div -5$

(e) $-20 \div 10$ (f) $-32 \div 8$ (g) $0 \div -4$ (h) $-16 \div -2$

(i) $36 \div -4$ (j) $-40 \div -5$ (k) $27 \div -9$ (l) $17 \div -17$

3 Calculate these.

(a) $\frac{1}{3} \times -12$ (b) $-24 \div 1$ (c) -5×6 (d) $-49 \div -7$

(e) -3×-9 (f) $(-2)^4$ (g) $\frac{-54}{-6}$ (h) $\frac{4}{-1}$

(i) $-20 \times \frac{1}{4}$ (j) $\frac{1}{3} \times -3$ (k) $-24 \times \frac{1}{4}$ (l) $(-1)^7$

4 Calculate these.

(a) $16 - (-2)$ (b) 16×-2 (c) $16 + (-2)$ (d) $-30 - (-12)$

(e) $-16 \div -8$ (f) $28 \div -7$ (g) $\frac{-2-12}{2}$ (h) $\frac{-6-(-14)}{4}$

(i) $\frac{-8+(-6)}{-8-(-6)}$ (j) $-5 \times 6 + (-7) + 8$

Lessons in Numeracy (Intermediate) © Longman (an imprint of Pearson Education) 2001

INTERMEDIATE ● HOMEWORK

7 Negative numbers 2

Do not use a calculator

1 Calculate these multiplications.

(a) -6×-4 (b) -7×5 (c) 3×-6 (d) -4×-8

(e) $(-6)^2$ (f) 4×7 (g) 0×5 (h) -7×0

(i) -3×8 (j) -7×-4 (k) $(-3)^2$ (l) -1×-11

2 Calculate these divisions.

(a) $16 \div -4$ (b) $36 \div 6$ (c) $-8 \div -2$ (d) $5 \div -5$

(e) $-20 \div 10$ (f) $-32 \div 8$ (g) $0 \div -4$ (h) $-16 \div -2$

(i) $36 \div -4$ (j) $-40 \div -5$ (k) $27 \div -9$ (l) $17 \div -17$

3 Calculate these.

(a) $\frac{1}{3} \times -12$ (b) $-24 \div 1$ (c) -5×6 (d) $-49 \div -7$

(e) -3×-9 (f) $(-2)^4$ (g) $\frac{-54}{-6}$ (h) $\frac{4}{-1}$

(i) $-20 \times \frac{1}{4}$ (j) $\frac{1}{3} \times -3$ (k) $-24 \times \frac{1}{4}$ (l) $(-1)^7$

4 Calculate these.

(a) $16 - (-2)$ (b) 16×-2 (c) $16 + (-2)$ (d) $-30 - (-12)$

(e) $-16 \div -8$ (f) $28 \div -7$ (g) $\frac{-2-12}{2}$ (h) $\frac{-6-(-14)}{4}$

(i) $\frac{-8+(-6)}{-8-(-6)}$ (j) $-5 \times 6 + (-7) + 8$

Lessons in Numeracy (Intermediate) © Longman (an imprint of Pearson Education) 2001

8 Order of operations

LESSON OBJECTIVES

● Use brackets and the hierarchy of operations

● Develop a range of strategies for mental calculation

WORKING INTERACTIVELY

● Discuss the need for being clear about what $4 \times 3 - 2$ means. Is it $12 - 2$ or 4×1? We all need to agree! The agreed meaning is $12 - 2$.

● Now discuss $20 - 5 \times 3$. This could be $20 - 15$ or 15×3. The agreed meaning is $20 - 15$.

● Give students this order for doing operations:

B   brackets
I   indices (x^2, x^3, etc.)
D   division
M   multiplication
A   addition   ⎫   working from
S   subtraction   ⎭   left to right

● Here are some examples:

$4 \times 8 - 3 \times 6 = 14$	Do multiplication before subtraction.
$5 \times 7 - (3 + 6) = 26$	Do the operation in the bracket first, then multiplication.
$7 + 3 \times 5^2 = 82$	Square the 5 first. Then do multiplication before addition.
$\dfrac{13 - 12 \div 4}{4 + 3 \times 2} = 1$	Do the top and the bottom of the fraction first.
$8 + 3 \times (-6) = -10$	Multiplication first.
$11 - 7 - 3 = 1$	Work from left to right.
$2 \times (-3)^3 + 3 \times (-5)^2 = 21$	Do powers first. Then multiplication before addition.

INDIVIDUAL WORK

Students work through the classwork sheet.

Review

Mark any classwork and review key strategies:

● Remind students of BIDMAS rule.

● Go over any examples which proved difficult and emphasise how the BIDMAS rule applies.

ANSWERS TO THE CLASSWORK SHEET

1 (a) 24   (b) 26   (c) 8
2 (a) 13   (b) 55   (c) 45
3 (a) 66   (b) 22   (c) 38   (d) –15   (e) 14   (f) 2
4 (a) 1   (b) 3   (c) 30   (d) 30   (e) 20   (f) 7
   (g) 52   (h) –8   (i) 1
5 (a) 43   (b) 75   (c) –60   (d) 4   (e) 45   (f) 16
6 (a) –2   (b) 4   (c) 5
7 (a) $(5 + 6) \times 3 = 33$ (b) $7 - (5 - 4) - 8 = -2$
   (c) $3 \times (9 - 4) \times 8 = 120$ (d) $(9 - (6 - 3)) \times 5 = 30$

HOMEWORK

Page
23

HOMEWORK
ANSWERS
Page
133

8 Order of operations

 **Do not use a calculator**

1 Work out these.

(a) $5 \times 7 - 11$

(b) $8 + 2 \times 9$

(c) $5 \times 4 - 4 \times 3$

2 Work out these.

(a) $8 \times (7 - 6) + 5$

(b) $8 \times 7 - 6 + 5$

(c) $8 \times 7 - (6 + 5)$

3 Work out these.

(a) $60 + 18 \div 3$

(b) $50 - 4 \times 7$

(c) $36 - 12 \div (-6)$

(d) $-18 + 24 \div 8$

(e) $20 - (-2) \times (-3)$

(f) $5 + (-15) \div 5$

4 Work out these.

(a) $21 - 16 + 4 - 8$

(b) $15 - (-3) + (-8) - 7$

(c) $60 \div 6 \times 3$

(d) $30 - 30 \div 5 + 1 \times 6$

(e) $19 - (5 + 3 \times (-2))$

(f) $(2 + (-5)) - 2 \times (-5)$

(g) $5 \times (8 - 4) + 8 \times 4$

(h) $-3 \times (5 + 4) - (-3) \times 5 + 4$

(i) $(3 + (-4)) \times (5 + (-6))$

5 Work out these.

(a) $2^4 + 3^3$

(b) 3×5^2

(c) $5 \times 2^3 - (5 \times 2)^2$

(d) $7 \times 4^2 - 4 \times 3^3$

(e) $(2^3 - 3) \times 3^2$

(f) $(7 - 5)^4$

6 Work out these.

(a) $\dfrac{3 \times 8 - 4}{8 - 9 \times 2}$

(b) $\dfrac{12 + 16 \div 4}{7 + 9 \div (-3)}$

(c) $\dfrac{9^2 - 4^2}{3^2 + 2^2}$

7 Put in brackets to make these statements true.

(a) $5 + 6 \times 3 = 33$

(b) $7 - 5 - 4 - 8 = -2$

(c) $3 \times 9 - 4 \times 8 = 120$

(d) $9 - 6 - 3 \times 5 = 30$

8 Order of operations

 **Do not use a calculator**

1 Work out the correct answer to each of these.

(a) $8 \times 7 - 6$

(b) $4 + 3 \times 6$

(c) $5 \times 8 - 6 \times 4$

(d) $12 - 6 \div 3$

2 Work out these.

(a) $9 \times (8 - 7) - 6$

(b) $9 \times 8 - 7 - 6$

(c) $9 \times 8 - (7 - 6)$

(d) $9 \times (8 - 7 - 6)$

3 Work out these.

(a) $15 + 18 \div (-3)$

(b) $-36 - 4 \times 5$

(c) $18 + (-25) \div (-5)$

(d) $18 + (-9) \div 9$

4 Work out these.

(a) $30 - 7 + 8 - 11$

(b) $23 + (-5) - (-9) - 4$

(c) $50 \div (-5) \times 5$

(d) $30 - 30 \div 10 + 2 \times 5$

(e) $-3 \times (10 - 4) + 5 \times 7$

(f) $(4 - 6) \times (6 + 5) - 3 \times 4 + 7$

5 Work out these.

(a) $3^2 - 4^2$

(b) $5 \times 2^5 - 3^3$

(c) $-2 \times 7^2 - 7 \times (-2)^3$

(d) $3 \times 5^3 - 5 \times (3^3 - 7) \times 2^3$

6 Work out these.

(a) $\dfrac{4 - 6 \times 9}{6 \times 4 + 1}$

(b) $\dfrac{16 - 32 \div 8}{25 \div 25 - 13}$

(c) $\dfrac{4^2 - 3^4}{3^2 + 2^2}$

(d) $\dfrac{-12 + \sqrt{12^2 - 4 \times (-3) \times 15}}{2 \times (-3)}$

7 Put in brackets to make these statements true.

(a) $4 \times 5 - 3 \times 8 - 7 - 2 = 15$

(b) $4 \times 5 - 3 \times 8 - 7 - 2 = 55$

(c) $4 \times 5 - 3 \times 8 - 7 - 2 = 11$

(d) $4 \times 5 - 3 \times 8 - 7 - 2 = -85$

9 Factors and divisibility tests

> **LESSON OBJECTIVES**
> ● Find all the factors of positive whole numbers
> ● Understand and use divisibility tests, so that division can be carried out more efficiently
> ● Develop a range of strategies for mental calculations

WORKING INTERACTIVELY

● Ask students to generate a list of multiples of 3 which is put on the board. Point out that the sum of the digits is always a multiple of 3.

● Repeat for multiples of 9, whose digit sums are always a multiple of 9.

● These facts provide a quick way of testing whether or not any number is exactly divisible by 3 or by 9.

● Ask students to suggest numbers to test for divisibility by 3 or by 9.

● What about divisibility tests for other numbers?

  2 It is an even number (ends in an even digit).

  4 *Either* halve the number and see if the result is even, *or* look at the last two digits. If they are a multiple of 4 then the number is.
  (If the penultimate digit is odd the last digit must be 2 or 6; if it is even the last digit must be 0, 4 or 8.)

  5 Number ends in 0 or 5.

  6 Divisible by 2 and by 3.

  8 Halve the number and see if the result is divisible by 4.

  There is no easily remembered test for 7.

● Point out that tests for other numbers can be built from these. For example, a number is divisible by 18 if it is divisible by 9 and even.

INDIVIDUAL WORK

Issue the classwork sheet and discuss how to fill it in. For example:

| 24 | 1, 2, 3, 4, 6, 8, 12, 24 | 8 |

Various strategies can be adopted to improve efficiency in completing the sheet:

● Every time you write down one factor (e.g. 2 in the example above) you can write down another factor (12), because 2 × 12 = 24. (This is not quite always true. Consider, for example, 6 being a factor of 36.)

● Work through the sheet, writing 2 against all the even numbers, 3 against all the multiples of 3, etc.

> The classwork sheet may seem to offer a repetitive exercise, but it provides students with insight into patterns of factors of numbers, as well as plenty of practice in dividing mentally. The completed sheet is needed for the homework and is also useful for lesson 10.

Review

Mark the factors sheet and review the divisibility tests.

HOMEWORK
Page
27

HOMEWORK
ANSWERS
Page
134

ANSWERS TO THE CLASSWORK SHEET

Number	Factors	Number of factors	Number	Factors	Number of factors
1	1	1	51	1, 3, 17, 51	4
2	1, 2	2	52	1, 2, 4, 13, 26, 52	6
3	1, 3	2	53	1, 53	2
4	1, 2, 4	3	54	1, 2, 3, 6, 9, 18, 27, 54	8
5	1, 5	2	55	1, 5, 11, 55	4
6	1, 2, 3, 6	4	56	1, 2, 4, 7, 8, 14, 28, 56	8
7	1, 7	2	57	1, 3, 19, 57	4
8	1, 2, 4, 8	4	58	1, 2, 29, 58	4
9	1, 3, 9	3	59	1, 59	2
10	1, 2, 5, 10	4	60	1, 2, 3, 4, 5, 6, 10, 12, 15, 20, 30, 60	12
11	1, 11	2	61	1, 61	2
12	1, 2, 3, 4, 6, 12	6	62	1, 2, 31, 62	4
13	1, 13	2	63	1, 3, 7, 9, 21, 63	6
14	1, 2, 7, 14	4	64	1, 2, 4, 8, 16, 32, 64	7
15	1, 3, 5, 15	4	65	1, 5, 13, 65	4
16	1, 2, 4, 8, 16	5	66	1, 2, 3, 6, 11, 22, 33, 66	8
17	1, 17	2	67	1, 67	2
18	1, 2, 3, 6, 9, 18	6	68	1, 2, 4, 17, 34, 68	6
19	1, 19	2	69	1, 3, 23, 69	4
20	1, 2, 4, 5, 10, 20	6	70	1, 2, 5, 7, 10, 14, 35, 70	8
21	1, 3, 7, 21	4	71	1, 71	2
22	1, 2, 11, 22	4	72	1, 2, 3, 4, 6, 8, 9, 12, 18, 24, 36, 72	12
23	1, 23	2	73	1, 73	2
24	1, 2, 3, 4, 6, 8, 12, 24	8	74	1, 2, 37, 74	4
25	1, 5, 25	3	75	1, 3, 5, 15, 25, 75	6
26	1, 2, 13, 26	4	76	1, 2, 4, 19, 38, 76	6
27	1, 3, 9, 27	4	77	1, 7, 11, 77	4
28	1, 2, 4, 7, 14, 28	6	78	1, 2, 3, 6, 13, 26, 39, 78	8
29	1, 29	2	79	1, 79	2
30	1, 2, 3, 5, 6, 10, 15, 30	8	80	1, 2, 4, 5, 8, 10, 16, 20, 40, 80	10
31	1, 31	2	81	1, 3, 9, 27, 81	5
32	1, 2, 4, 8, 16, 32	6	82	1, 2, 41, 82	4
33	1, 3, 11, 33	4	83	1, 83	2
34	1, 2, 17, 34	4	84	1, 2, 3, 4, 6, 7, 12, 14, 21, 28, 42, 84	12
35	1, 5, 7, 35	4	85	1, 5, 17, 85	4
36	1, 2, 3, 4, 6, 9, 12, 18, 36	9	86	1, 2, 43, 86	4
37	1, 37	2	87	1, 3, 29, 87	4
38	1, 2, 19, 38	4	88	1, 2, 4, 8, 11, 22, 44, 88	8
39	1, 3, 13, 39	4	89	1, 89	2
40	1, 2, 4, 5, 8, 10, 20, 40	8	90	1, 2, 3, 5, 6, 9, 10, 15, 18, 30, 45, 90	12
41	1, 41	2	91	1, 7, 13, 91	4
42	1, 2, 3, 6, 7, 14, 21, 42	8	92	1, 2, 4, 23, 46, 92	6
43	1, 43	2	93	1, 3, 31, 93	4
44	1, 2, 4, 11, 22, 44	6	94	1, 2, 47, 94	4
45	1, 3, 5, 9, 15, 45	6	95	1, 5, 19, 95	4
46	1, 2, 23, 46	4	96	1, 2, 3, 4, 6, 8, 12, 16, 24, 32, 48, 96	12
47	1, 47	2	97	1, 97	2
48	1, 2, 3, 4, 6, 8, 12, 16, 24, 48	10	98	1, 2, 7, 14, 49, 98	6
49	1, 7, 49	3	99	1, 3, 9, 11, 33, 99	6
50	1, 2, 5, 10, 25, 50	6	100	1, 2, 4, 5, 10, 20, 25, 50, 100	9

 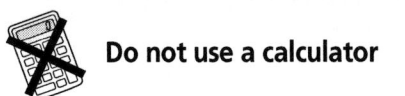
9 Factors and divisibility tests

Number	Factors	Number of factors	Number	Factors	Number of factors
1			51		
2			52		
3			53		
4			54		
5			55		
6			56		
7			57		
8			58		
9			59		
10			60		
11			61		
12			62		
13			63		
14			64		
15			65		
16			66		
17			67		
18			68		
19			69		
20			70		
21			71		
22			72		
23			73		
24			74		
25			75		
26			76		
27			77		
28			78		
29			79		
30			80		
31			81		
32			82		
33			83		
34			84		
35			85		
36			86		
37			87		
38			88		
39			89		
40			90		
41			91		
42			92		
43			93		
44			94		
45			95		
46			96		
47			97		
48			98		
49			99		
50			100		

Lessons in Numeracy (Intermediate) © Longman (an imprint of Pearson Education) 2001

9 Factors and divisibility tests

 Do not use a calculator

Use the factors sheet you completed in the lesson to help you answer these questions.

1 Look at this list of numbers:

566   732   351   756

858   747   594   825

(a) Which of the numbers are divisible by 9?

(b) Which of the numbers are divisible by 6?

2 Look at this list of numbers:

243   324   514   718

276   742   987   788

(a) Which of the numbers are divisible by 4?

(b) Which of the numbers are divisible by 3?

(c) Use your answers to (a) and (b) to write down the numbers that are divisible by 12.

3 (a) Suggest a divisibility test for 15.

(b) Which of these numbers are divisible by 15?

75 126 735 800 1105 1230

1205 1305 1356 12 345

4 Which of these numbers are divisible by 24?

144 224 324 512 624 768

5 List all the numbers up to 100 with *exactly* 2 factors. These are called **prime numbers**.

6 List all the numbers up to 100 with an *odd* numbers of factors. These are called **square numbers**.

7 List all the numbers up to 100 with *exactly* 3 factors. Try to describe these numbers.

8 (a) Write down the smallest number which has

(i) 4 factors

(ii) 6 factors

(iii) 8 factors

(iv) 10 factors

(v) 12 factors

(b) Find the smallest number which has 14 factors.

10 Primes, squares, square roots and cubes

LESSON OBJECTIVES

● Understand and use prime numbers

● Understand and use square numbers and square roots

● Understand and use cube numbers and cube roots

● Recall integer squares from 2 × 2 to 15 × 15 and the corresponding square roots

● Recall the cubes of 2, 3, 4, 5 and 10

WORKING INTERACTIVELY

The completed factors sheet from lesson 9 is useful.

● A prime number has exactly 2 factors (1 and the number itself).
Students should have listed the 25 primes less than 100 in the homework for lesson 9:
2, 3, 5, 7, 11, 13, 17, 19, 23, 29, 31, 37, 41, 43, 47, 53, 59, 61, 67, 71, 73, 79, 83, 89, 97

● A square number is the result of multiplying a number by itself.
It can be thought of as the area of a square with a side equal to a whole number. In lesson 9 homework it was noted that only *square numbers* have an *odd* number of factors.

● Ask students to list the first 15 square numbers:
$1^2 = 1$, $2^2 = 4$, $3^2 = 9$, $4^2 = 16$, $5^2 = 25$, $6^2 = 36$, $7^2 = 49$, $8^2 = 64$, $9^2 = 81$, $10^2 = 100$, $11^2 = 121$, $12^2 = 144$, $13^2 = 169$, $14^2 = 196$, $15^2 = 225$
Point out to students that they are expected to recognise these.

● Obtaining a square root is the reverse process to obtaining a square.

● The square root of a number can be thought of as the side of the square whose area is that number,
e.g. $\sqrt{81} = 9$, $\sqrt{144} = 12$

● Note that numbers other than whole numbers can be squared.
For example $(3\frac{1}{2})^2 = 12\frac{1}{4}$, $(1.2)^2 = 1.44$. The result of squaring a number that is not a whole number is not usually called a square number, but it is sometimes called a **perfect square**.

● To find the (approximate) square root of a number other than a perfect square, a calculator is required.

● Note that the square root of 81 is 9 or −9, because $−9 \times −9 = 81$.
Similarly, the square root of 196 is 14 or −14.
The notation $\sqrt{196}$ usually means the positive square root (14, in this case). To indicate the other square root, use $−\sqrt{196}$.

● A cube number is the result of multiplying a number by itself 'three times'.
It can be thought of as the volume of a cube with edge length equal to a whole number.

● Ask students to generate the first ten cube numbers:
$1^3 = 1$, $2^3 = 8$, $3^3 = 27$, $4^3 = 64$, $5^3 = 125$, $6^3 = 216$, $7^3 = 343$, $8^3 = 512$, $9^3 = 729$, $10^3 = 1000$

● Obtaining a cube root is the reverse process to obtaining a cube.
The cube root of a number can be thought of as the edge of the cube whose volume is that number,
e.g. $\sqrt[3]{64} = 4$, $\sqrt[3]{343} = 7$

● *Finding more prime numbers*
How can we find out whether 113 is prime?
Discuss the fact that you only have to test prime numbers (any other divisor would itself contain a prime number).
Discuss the fact that you only have to test 2, 3, 5 and 7, because $11^2 = 121$, which is bigger than 113. (Factors occur in pairs and one number in the pair must always be less than $\sqrt{113}$.)
113 is clearly not divisible by 2 or 5.
It is not divisible by 3, because its digit sum is 5, which is not divisible by 3.
Divide by 7. 113 ÷ 7 = 16 r 1. So 113 is not divisible by 7.
So 113 is prime.

● Ask students to suggest another number between 100 and 200, to test whether or not it is prime.

INDIVIDUAL WORK

Set students the task of finding all the prime numbers between 100 and 200. They could share out the work, with one group working on 101 to 110, another on 111 to 120, and so on.

The are 21 primes between 100 and 200:

101, 103, 107, 109, 113, 127, 131, 137, 139, 149, 151, 157, 163, 167, 173, 179, 181, 191, 193, 197, 199

Review

Discuss the work done by students in finding the prime numbers between 100 and 200. Check any misconceptions.

Check that the terms, square, cube, square root, cube root, are understood, because they are needed for the homework.

HOMEWORK

Page
30

**HOMEWORK
ANSWERS**
Page
134

10 Primes, squares, square roots and cubes

 **Do not use a calculator**

1 Look at these numbers.

4   9   24   29   44   49   64   69   84   89

(a) Which of the numbers are primes?

(b) Which of the numbers are squares?

(c) Which of the numbers are cubes?

2 Write down the value of these.

(a) 7^2 (b) 11^2 (c) 14^2 (d) $\sqrt{81}$

(e) $\sqrt{144}$ (f) $\sqrt{169}$ (g) 4^3 (h) 7^3

(i) 9^3 (j) $\sqrt[3]{27}$ (k) $\sqrt[3]{1000}$ (l) $\sqrt[3]{125}$

3 Give a reason why each of the following numbers is not prime.

(a) 57   (b) 1452   (c) 795

(d) 91   (e) 143   (f) 3483

4 (a) Work out 17^2

(b) Explain why you do not have to consider factors bigger than 13 to show that 211 is a prime number.

(c) Show that 211 is a prime number.

5 Find the next three prime numbers after 211.

Lessons in Numeracy (Intermediate) © Longman (an imprint of Pearson Education) 2001

INTERMEDIATE ● HOMEWORK

10 Primes, squares, square roots and cubes

Do not use a calculator

1 Look at these numbers.

4   9   24   29   44   49   64   69   84   89

(a) Which of the numbers are primes?

(b) Which of the numbers are squares?

(c) Which of the numbers are cubes?

2 Write down the value of these.

(a) 7^2 (b) 11^2 (c) 14^2 (d) $\sqrt{81}$

(e) $\sqrt{144}$ (f) $\sqrt{169}$ (g) 4^3 (h) 7^3

(i) 9^3 (j) $\sqrt[3]{27}$ (k) $\sqrt[3]{1000}$ (l) $\sqrt[3]{125}$

3 Give a reason why each of the following numbers is not prime.

(a) 57 (b) 1452 (c) 795

(d) 91 (e) 143 (f) 3483

4 (a) Work out 17^2

(b) Explain why you do not have to consider factors bigger than 13 to show that 211 is a prime number.

(c) Show that 211 is a prime number.

5 Find the next three prime numbers after 211.

Lessons in Numeracy (Intermediate) © Longman (an imprint of Pearson Education) 2001

11 Prime factorisation

LESSON OBJECTIVES

● Find the prime factor decomposition of positive integers
● Use prime factor decomposition to find the highest common factor and the lowest common multiple of sets of positive integers

WORKING INTERACTIVELY

Explain what it means to write a number as the **product of prime factors**.

e.g $24 = 2 \times 2 \times 2 \times 3 = 2^3 \times 3$ $21 = 3 \times 7$
$30 = 2 \times 3 \times 5$ $17 = 17$

This process is called **prime factorisation** or **prime factor decomposition**.

INDIVIDUAL WORK (10 MINUTES)

Students work through the *Prime factorisation* section of the classwork sheet.

WORKING INTERACTIVELY

● Use the prime factorisation of 12 and 18 to find the largest number which is a factor of both of them (the **highest common factor**) and also the smallest number which is a multiple of both of them (the **lowest common multiple**).

$12 = 2 \times \mathbf{2} \times \mathbf{3}$	$12 = \mathbf{2} \times \mathbf{2} \times 3$
$18 = 2 \times \mathbf{3} \times 3$	$18 = 2 \times \mathbf{3} \times \mathbf{3}$
So highest common factor is $\mathbf{2} \times \mathbf{3} = 6$.	Lowest common multiple is $\mathbf{2} \times \mathbf{2} \times \mathbf{3} \times \mathbf{3} = 36$.

● Use the prime factorisation of 15 and 25 to find the highest common factor and the lowest common multiple.

$15 = 3 \times \mathbf{5}$	$15 = \mathbf{3} \times 5$
$25 = 5 \times \mathbf{5}$	$25 = \mathbf{5} \times \mathbf{5}$
So highest common factor is 5.	Lowest common multiple is $\mathbf{3} \times \mathbf{5} \times \mathbf{5} = 75$.

● Do the same with 72 and 126.
$72 = 2^3 \times 3^2$ and $126 = 2 \times 3^2 \times 7$ and so highest common factor is $2 \times 3^2 = 18$ and lowest common multiple is $2^3 \times 3^2 \times 7 = 504$.

● Do the same with 375 and 600.
$375 = 3 \times 5^3$ and $600 = 2^3 \times 3 \times 5^2$ and so highest common factor is $3 \times 5^2 = 75$ and lowest common multiple is $2^3 \times 3 \times 5^3 = 3000$.

INDIVIDUAL WORK

Students work through the *Highest common factors and lowest common multiples* section of the classwork sheet.

Review

Mark classwork and review strategies, ensuring that students are clear about the process of obtaining highest common factors and lowest common multiples.

ANSWERS TO THE CLASSWORK SHEET

Prime factorisation

1 $12 = 2^2 \times 3$ **2** $50 = 2 \times 5^2$ **3** $9 = 3^2$

4 $8 = 2^3$ **5** $72 = 2^3 \times 3^2$ **6** $75 = 3 \times 5^2$

7 $17 = 17$ **8** $36 = 2^2 \times 3^2$ **9** $49 = 7^2$

10 $56 = 2^3 \times 7$ **11** $35 = 5 \times 7$ **12** $32 = 2^5$

13 $53 = 53$ **14** $86 = 2 \times 43$ **15** $69 = 3 \times 23$

16 $144 = 2^4 \times 3^2$ **17** $126 = 2 \times 3^2 \times 7$ **18** $375 = 3 \times 5^3$

19 $600 = 2^3 \times 3 \times 5^2$ **20** $1001 = 7 \times 11 \times 13$

Highest common factors and lowest common multiples

1 $6 = 2 \times 3, \ 9 = 3 \times 3$
Highest common factor is 3. Lowest common multiple is $2 \times 3 \times 3 = 18$.

2 $12 = 2 \times 2 \times 3, \ 16 = 2 \times 2 \times 2 \times 2$
Highest common factor is $2 \times 2 = 4$. Lowest common multiple is $2 \times 2 \times 2 \times 2 \times 3 = 48$.

3 $15 = 3 \times 5, \ 20 = 2 \times 2 \times 5$
Highest common factor is 5. Lowest common multiple is $2 \times 2 \times 3 \times 5 = 60$.

4 $8 = 2 \times 2 \times 2, \ 12 = 2 \times 2 \times 3$
Highest common factor is $2 \times 2 = 4$. Lowest common multiple is $2 \times 2 \times 2 \times 3 = 24$.

5 $28 = 2 \times 2 \times 7, \ 42 = 2 \times 3 \times 7$
Highest common factor is $2 \times 7 = 14$. Lowest common multiple is $2 \times 2 \times 3 \times 7 = 84$.

6 $36 = 2 \times 2 \times 3 \times 3, \ 54 = 2 \times 3 \times 3 \times 3$
Highest common factor is $2 \times 3 \times 3 = 18$. Lowest common multiple is $2 \times 2 \times 3 \times 3 \times 3 = 108$.

7 $68 = 2 \times 2 \times 17, \ 51 = 3 \times 17$
Highest common factor is 17. Lowest common multiple is $2 \times 2 \times 3 \times 17 = 204$.

8 $56 = 2 \times 2 \times 2 \times 7, \ 84 = 2 \times 2 \times 3 \times 7$
Highest common factor is $2 \times 2 \times 7 = 28$. Lowest common multiple is $2 \times 2 \times 2 \times 3 \times 7 = 168$.

9 $60 = 2 \times 2 \times 3 \times 5, \ 144 = 2 \times 2 \times 2 \times 2 \times 3 \times 3$
Highest common factor is $2 \times 2 \times 3 = 12$. Lowest common multiple is $2 \times 2 \times 2 \times 2 \times 3 \times 3 \times 5 = 720$.

HOMEWORK
Page
37

HOMEWORK ANSWERS
Page
134

11 Prime factorisation

Do not use a calculator

Prime factorisation

Write each of these numbers as the product of prime factors.

1 12	**2** 50	**3** 9	**4** 8
5 72	**6** 75	**7** 17	**8** 36
9 49	**10** 56	**11** 35	**12** 32
13 53	**14** 86	**15** 69	**16** 144
17 126	**18** 375	**19** 600	**20** 1001

Highest common factors and lowest common multiples

Find the highest common factor and lowest common
multiple of each of these pairs of numbers.

1 6 and 9 **2** 12 and 16 **3** 15 and 20

4 8 and 12 **5** 28 and 42 **6** 36 and 54

7 68 and 51 **8** 56 and 84 **9** 60 and 144

Lessons in Numeracy (Intermediate) © Longman (an imprint of Pearson Education) 2001

33

Prime factorisation

Do as many of these questions as you can without a calculator

1 Express each of these numbers as the product of prime factors.

(a) 20   (b) 40

(c) 81   (d) 105

(e) 238   (f) 231

(g) 96   (h) 273

2 Find the smallest number which is a multiple of *both* numbers in each pair.

(a) 6 and 16

(b) 8 and 18

(c) 21 and 35

(d) 84 and 147

(e) 18 and 30

(f) 45 and 75

3 Find the largest number which is a factor of *both* numbers in each pair.

(a) 24 and 80

(b) 56 and 84

(c) 42 and 70

(d) 60 and 96

(e) 567 and 729

(f) 147 and 343

4 In each of these, guess the number from the clues given.

(a) I am even and I am prime.

(b) I have exactly five factors and I am less than 50.

(c) I am less than 40 and I am a multiple of both 2 and 3. If I was two less, I would be square.

(d) I am less than 50, and I am a square number, and I can be made by adding two other square numbers together.

5 (a) Express 756 as the product of prime factors.

(b) What is the smallest number which 756 must be multiplied by to make a square number?

6 (a) Express 14 700 as the product of prime factors.

(b) Find the smallest square number which is a multiple of 14 700.

12 Fractions of quantities

> **LESSON OBJECTIVES**
> ● Calculate a given fraction of a given quantity
> ● Understand and use fractions as multiplicative inverses
> ● Multiply a given fraction by an integer
> ● Use inverse operations and suitable techniques to solve problems

WORKING INTERACTIVELY

● How do we find $\frac{2}{3}$ of 54?
These methods are equivalent and either is useful, depending on the numbers.
Find $\frac{1}{3}$ of 54 by dividing by 3, and then multiply by 2.

$$\left(\frac{54}{3} \times 2 = 18 \times 2 = 36\right)$$

or First multiply 54 by 2 and then divide by 3.

$$\left(\frac{54 \times 2}{3} = \frac{108}{3} = 36\right)$$

● Discuss $\frac{3}{4}$ of 24 in a similar way.

$$\frac{24}{4} \times 3 = 6 \times 3 = 18 \quad \text{or} \quad \frac{24 \times 3}{4} = \frac{72}{4} = 18$$

● What is $\frac{1}{3}$ of $\frac{3}{5}$ of 30?

One obvious approach is to find $\frac{3}{5}$ of 30 (which is 18) and then $\frac{1}{3}$ of this (which is 6).

Or, it can be observed that this is equivalent to $\frac{1}{5}$ of 30.

So, $\frac{1}{3}$ of $\frac{3}{5} = \frac{1}{3} \times \frac{3}{5} = \frac{1}{5}$

INDIVIDUAL WORK (10 MINUTES)

Students work through the *Numbers* section of the classwork sheet.

WORKING INTERACTIVELY

● I give you $\frac{1}{4}$ of my bar of chocolate. What fraction of the bar do I have left?

Practise this skill with other fractions:

$\frac{2}{3}$ $\frac{3}{5}$ $\frac{3}{10}$ $\frac{3}{8}$

● In a bag there are some cubes. Half of the cubes are blue and there are 6 blue cubes.

How many cubes are there altogether?
(12 cubes altogether)

● Set similar problems.

$\frac{1}{4}$ of the cubes are red and there are 8 red cubes.
(32 cubes altogether)

$\frac{1}{3}$ of the cubes are green and there are 7 green cubes.
(21 cubes altogether)

$\frac{1}{5}$ of the cubes are yellow and there are 6 yellow cubes.
(30 cubes altogether)

$\frac{1}{10}$ of the cubes are white and there are 5 white cubes.
(50 cubes altogether)

● Now consider problems like this.

$\frac{3}{4}$ of the cubes are blue and there are 12 blue cubes.
How many cubes are there altogether?
Here is one method.

4	4
	4

So $\frac{1}{4}$ of the cubes is 4 cubes.

So the bag contains 16 cubes.

● Set similar problems.

$\frac{2}{3}$ of the cubes are red and there are 10 red cubes.
(15 cubes altogether)

$\frac{2}{5}$ of the cubes are green and there are 8 green cubes.
(20 cubes altogether)

$\frac{3}{8}$ of the cubes are yellow and there are 12 yellow cubes. (32 cubes altogether)

● Now move away from cubes.

$\frac{3}{5}$ of the students in a class are girls. There are 18 girls.
How many students altogether? (30 students)

And so on.

INDIVIDUAL WORK

Students work through the *Quantities* section of the classwork sheet.

Review

Mark classwork and discuss strategies for the questions students found difficult.

ANSWERS TO THE CLASSWORK SHEET

Numbers

1 (a) £8   (b) £16   (c) £18   (d) £55

2 (a) 27   (b) 50   (c) 60   (d) 12   (e) 50   (f) 49

3 63

4 20

5 9

6 50

7 270

8 214

9 108

10 36

11 96

12 48

Quantities

1 $\frac{5}{9}$

2 72 teachers

3 12 sweets

4 9 women

5 (a) 400   (b) 360   (c) More swim   (d) 2/3

6 (a) 63   (b) 45   (c) 32   (d) 225   (e) 324   (f) 132

HOMEWORK

Page 38

HOMEWORK ANSWERS

Page 134

12 Fractions of quantities

 **Do not use a calculator**

Numbers

Calculate the answers in questions 1 to 10.

1 (a) $\frac{1}{4}$ of £32   **(b)** $\frac{1}{3}$ of £48   **(c)** $\frac{1}{5}$ of £90   **(d)** $\frac{1}{6}$ of £330

2 (a) $\frac{3}{4}$ of 36   **(b)** $\frac{2}{3}$ of 75   **(c)** $\frac{2}{5}$ of 150   **(d)** $\frac{4}{9}$ of 27

    (e) $\frac{5}{6}$ of 60   **(f)** $\frac{7}{8}$ of 56

3 $\frac{7}{10}$ of 90   **4** $\frac{4}{9}$ of 45   **5** $\frac{3}{100}$ of 300   **6** $\frac{2}{5}$ of 125

7 $\frac{3}{8}$ of 720   **8** $\frac{2}{3}$ of 321   **9** $144 \times \frac{3}{4}$ **10** $63 \times \frac{4}{7}$

11 72 is $\frac{3}{4}$ of a number. What is the number?   **12** What is $\frac{2}{3}$ of $\frac{4}{5}$ of 90?

Quantities

1 In a bag there are black and orange cubes. $\frac{4}{9}$ of the cubes are black. What fraction are orange?

2 Of the teachers in a school, $\frac{5}{8}$ wear glasses. 45 teachers wear glasses. How many teachers are there in the school?

3 Ann gave her brother 8 sweets. She still had $\frac{3}{5}$ of the bag left for herself. How many sweets did she have left?

4 $\frac{3}{8}$ of the actors in a play are women. There are 15 men acting in the play. How many women are acting in the play?

5 A sports club has 600 members. $\frac{2}{3}$ of the members swim and $\frac{3}{5}$ of them use weights.
   (a) How many members swim?   **(b)** How many members use weights?
   (c) Do more members swim or use weights? **(d)** Which fraction is bigger: $\frac{2}{3}$ or $\frac{3}{5}$?

6 For each of these statements find the number.
   (a) $\frac{1}{7}$ of a number is 9   **(b)** $\frac{2}{5}$ of a number is 18   **(c)** $\frac{7}{8}$ of a number is 28
   (d) $\frac{4}{9}$ of a number is 100   **(e)** $\frac{3}{4}$ of a number is 243   **(f)** $\frac{6}{11}$ of a number is 96

12 Fractions of quantities

Do not use a calculator

Calculate the answers in questions 1 to 10.

1   (a) $\frac{1}{3}$ of £27   (b) $\frac{1}{4}$ of £52

    (c) $\frac{1}{6}$ of £96   (d) $\frac{1}{5}$ of £325

2   (a) $\frac{2}{5}$ of 75   (b) $\frac{2}{3}$ of 150

    (c) $\frac{4}{7}$ of 21   (d) $\frac{5}{6}$ of 36

    (e) $\frac{3}{8}$ of 48   (f) $\frac{3}{8}$ of 128

3   (a) $\frac{3}{10}$ of 130   (b) $\frac{3}{5}$ of 45

    (c) $\frac{7}{100}$ of 500   (d) $\frac{3}{5}$ of 225

    (e) $\frac{5}{8}$ of 104   (f) $\frac{2}{3}$ of 360

    (g) $\frac{3}{4}$ of 2000

4 $42 \times \frac{3}{7}$

5   60 is $\frac{2}{3}$ of a number. What is the number?

6   What is $\frac{2}{5}$ of $\frac{3}{4}$ of 100?

7   In a bag there are blue and yellow cubes. $\frac{7}{12}$ of the cubes are blue. What fraction are yellow?

8   Of the people at a concert, $\frac{7}{10}$ were teenagers. There were 700 teenagers at the concert. How many people were at the concert altogether?

9   Darren gives his sister 5 sweets. He still has $\frac{3}{4}$ of the bag left for himself. How many sweets does Darren have left?

10   In a village badminton club there are 12 females. They make up $\frac{2}{5}$ of the club. How many males are there in the club?

11   84 people were asked what pets they had. $\frac{3}{4}$ said they had a hamster and $\frac{5}{7}$ said they had a goldfish.

    (a) How many people said they had a hamster?

    (b) How many people said they had a goldfish?

    (c) Which pet did more people have?

    (d) Which fraction is bigger: $\frac{3}{4}$ or $\frac{5}{7}$?

12   For each of these statements find the number.

    (a) $\frac{1}{4}$ of a number is 5

    (b) $\frac{2}{3}$ of a number is 14

    (c) $\frac{2}{5}$ of a number is 12

    (d) $\frac{5}{6}$ of a number is 35

    (e) $\frac{3}{4}$ of a number is 72

    (f) $\frac{4}{7}$ of a number is 68

13   Lorraine earns £800 each month. Each month, a quarter of her income is used to pay the rent for her flat. One fifth of the income that she has left after paying the rent is put into a savings account. What fraction of her monthly income is left after the above amounts have been taken away?

13

Equivalent fractions and ordering fractions

LESSON OBJECTIVES

● Understand equivalent fractions
● Express a given number as a fraction of another
● Simplify a fraction by cancelling down
● Order fractions by re-writing them with a common denominator

---

WORKING INTERACTIVELY

● Write on the board a lot of fractions equal to $\frac{2}{3}$ and ask what they have in common.

● Reverse the process. What is the simplest fraction equal to each of these?

$\frac{20}{24}$ $\left(\frac{5}{6}\right)$

$\frac{15}{45}$ $\left(\frac{1}{3}\right)$

$\frac{250}{400}$ $\left(\frac{5}{8}\right)$

● Introduce the terms **simplest form**, **numerator** and **denominator**.

● Discuss questions like these.

What fraction of 50 is 15? $\left(\frac{15}{50} = \frac{3}{10}\right)$

What fraction of an hour is 5 minutes? $\left(\frac{5}{60} = \frac{1}{12}\right)$

What fraction of a metre is 35 cm? $\left(\frac{35}{100} = \frac{7}{20}\right)$

INDIVIDUAL WORK

Students work through questions 1 to 7 of the classwork sheet.

WORKING INTERACTIVELY

● Which is bigger: $\frac{2}{5}$ or $\frac{3}{5}$? $\left(\frac{3}{5}\right)$

● Which is bigger: $\frac{1}{4}$ or $\frac{1}{5}$? $\left(\frac{1}{4}\right)$

● Ask students to list these fractions in order of size, with the smallest first:

$\frac{1}{5}$ $\frac{1}{8}$ $\frac{1}{3}$ $\frac{1}{2}$ $\frac{1}{10}$ $\frac{1}{100}$ $\frac{1}{4}$ $\left(\frac{1}{100} \quad \frac{1}{10} \quad \frac{1}{8} \quad \frac{1}{5} \quad \frac{1}{4} \quad \frac{1}{3} \quad \frac{1}{2}\right)$

● Which is bigger: $\frac{7}{10}$ or $\frac{7}{100}$?

$\left(\frac{1}{10}$ is bigger than $\frac{1}{100}$, so $\frac{7}{10}$ is bigger than $\frac{7}{100}\right)$

● Ask students to list these sets of fractions in order of size, with the smallest first:

$\frac{5}{12}$ $\frac{5}{9}$ $\frac{5}{7}$ $\frac{5}{11}$ $\frac{5}{17}$ $\left(\frac{5}{17} \quad \frac{5}{12} \quad \frac{5}{11} \quad \frac{5}{9} \quad \frac{5}{7}\right)$

● Then ask students to draw a line on squared paper which is 12 squares long.

Ask them which fraction is bigger: $\frac{2}{3}$ or $\frac{3}{4}$. Discuss how the line can help.

● Refer back to the first part of this lesson on equivalent fractions. Point out the need to make denominators equal in order to compare the size of fractions.

● List these fractions in order of size, smallest first.

$\frac{1}{5}$ $\frac{3}{10}$ $\frac{1}{4}$ $\left(\frac{1}{5} \quad \frac{1}{4} \quad \frac{3}{10}\right)$

● Remind students of the symbols < and >.

● Discuss how to find a fraction between two given fractions.

To find a fraction between $\frac{3}{4}$ and $\frac{7}{8}$:

Change to a common denominator: $\frac{6}{8}$ and $\frac{7}{8}$

Either a fraction between these is $\frac{6\frac{1}{2}}{8} = \frac{13}{16}$

or $\frac{6}{8} = \frac{12}{16}$ and $\frac{7}{8} = \frac{14}{16}$

To find a fraction between $\frac{5}{6}$ and $\frac{11}{12}$:

Change to a common denominator: $\frac{10}{12}$ and $\frac{11}{12}$

Either a fraction between these is $\frac{10\frac{1}{2}}{12} = \frac{21}{24}$

or $\frac{10}{12} = \frac{20}{24}$ and $\frac{11}{12} = \frac{22}{24}$

INDIVIDUAL WORK

Students work through the remainder of the questions of the classwork sheet.

Review

Review vocabulary: **equivalent fractions, numerator, denominator, cancelling, simplest form.**

Review key strategies:

● Fractions are equivalent (stay the same) if you:
  multiply numerator and denominator by the same number
  divide numerator and denominator by the same number.

● To find what fraction one number (A) is of another (B), write down $\frac{A}{B}$ and cancel down. The numbers must be in the same units (e.g. minutes, millilitres).

● Ordering fractions with the same denominator: $\frac{2}{7} < \frac{4}{7}$, etc.

● Ordering fractions with the same numerator $\frac{2}{7} < \frac{2}{5}$, etc.

● Ordering fractions by using a common denominator $\frac{1}{3} < \frac{3}{8}$, because $\frac{8}{24} < \frac{9}{24}$.

● Finding a fraction between two fractions,

  e.g. between $\frac{1}{3}$ and $\frac{3}{8}$:

  $\frac{8\frac{1}{2}}{24} = \frac{17}{48}$, or compare $\frac{1}{3} = \frac{16}{48}$ and $\frac{3}{8} = \frac{18}{48}$.

ANSWERS TO THE CLASSWORK SHEET

1 (a) 3 (b) 25 (c) 8 (d) 6 (e) 7 (f) 8

2 $\frac{24}{63} = \frac{8}{21}$ $\left(\frac{16}{36} = \frac{40}{90} = \frac{48}{108} = \frac{80}{120} = \frac{4}{9}\right)$

3 $\frac{12}{30} = \frac{36}{90}$, $\frac{12}{21} = \frac{32}{56}$

4 (a) $\frac{3}{4}$ (b) $\frac{2}{3}$ (c) $\frac{1}{6}$ (d) $\frac{2}{5}$

5 (a) $\frac{1}{4}$ (b) $\frac{3}{8}$ (c) $\frac{1}{5}$ (d) $\frac{1}{16}$

6 $\frac{7}{10}$

7 (a) $\frac{5}{12}$ (b) 9 minutes

8 (a) $\frac{1}{11}, \frac{2}{11}, \frac{4}{11}, \frac{8}{11}$ (b) $\frac{1}{9}, \frac{1}{6}, \frac{1}{5}, \frac{1}{2}$

  (c) $\frac{3}{11}, \frac{3}{8}, \frac{3}{5}, \frac{3}{4}$ (d) $\frac{1}{6}, \frac{1}{4}, \frac{1}{3}, \frac{3}{8}, \frac{5}{12}$

9 (a) > (b) < (c) = (d) > (e) >
  (f) > (g) = (h) = (i) < (j) <

10 (a) e.g. $\frac{5}{16}$ (b) e.g. $\frac{31}{40}$ (c) e.g. $\frac{97}{168}$

HOMEWORK

Page 42

HOMEWORK ANSWERS

Page 134

13 Equivalent fractions and ordering fractions

Do not use a calculator

1 What number does the ∗ replace in each of these?

(a) $\dfrac{1}{8}=\dfrac{*}{24}$ (b) $\dfrac{3}{5}=\dfrac{15}{*}$ (c) $\dfrac{2}{3}=\dfrac{*}{12}$ (d) $\dfrac{5}{*}=\dfrac{20}{24}$ (e) $\dfrac{*}{10}=\dfrac{35}{50}$ (f) $\dfrac{10}{16}=\dfrac{5}{*}$

2 Which of these is the odd one out?

$\dfrac{16}{36}$ $\dfrac{40}{90}$ $\dfrac{24}{63}$ $\dfrac{48}{108}$ $\dfrac{80}{180}$

3 Say which of these fractions are equal.

$\dfrac{12}{30}$ $\dfrac{30}{120}$ $\dfrac{12}{21}$ $\dfrac{36}{90}$ $\dfrac{36}{120}$ $\dfrac{32}{56}$ $\dfrac{56}{120}$

4 Write each of these times as fractions of 1 hour, in their simplest form.

(a) 45 minutes   (b) 40 minutes   (c) 10 minutes   (d) 24 minutes

5 Write each of these masses as fractions of 2 kg, in their simplest form.

(a) 500 g   (b) 750 g   (c) 400 g   (d) 12.5 g

6 What fraction of 80 is 56?

7 (a) What fraction of a turn is 150°?

(b) How many minutes does it take the minute hand of a clock to turn through $\dfrac{3}{5}$ of a right angle?

8 In each of these parts, arrange the fractions in order of size, smallest first.

(a) $\dfrac{4}{11}$ $\dfrac{2}{11}$ $\dfrac{8}{11}$ $\dfrac{1}{11}$ (b) $\dfrac{1}{5}$ $\dfrac{1}{2}$ $\dfrac{1}{6}$ $\dfrac{1}{9}$ (c) $\dfrac{3}{4}$ $\dfrac{3}{8}$ $\dfrac{3}{5}$ $\dfrac{3}{11}$ (d) $\dfrac{1}{3}$ $\dfrac{3}{8}$ $\dfrac{5}{12}$ $\dfrac{1}{6}$ $\dfrac{1}{4}$

9 Put one of the signs <, = > between each pair of fractions to make a correct statement.

(a) $\dfrac{1}{4}$ and $\dfrac{1}{5}$ (b) $\dfrac{2}{5}$ and $\dfrac{3}{7}$ (c) $\dfrac{4}{10}$ and $\dfrac{2}{5}$ (d) $\dfrac{2}{3}$ and $\dfrac{7}{12}$ (e) $\dfrac{5}{8}$ and $\dfrac{6}{10}$

(f) $\dfrac{6}{7}$ and $\dfrac{4}{5}$ (g) $\dfrac{3}{10}$ and $\dfrac{6}{20}$ (h) $\dfrac{4}{6}$ and $\dfrac{6}{9}$ (i) $\dfrac{5}{9}$ and $\dfrac{4}{7}$ (j) $\dfrac{3}{4}$ and $\dfrac{8}{10}$

10 (a) Write down a fraction between $\dfrac{1}{4}$ and $\dfrac{3}{8}$.

(b) Write down a fraction between $\dfrac{3}{4}$ and $\dfrac{4}{5}$.

(c) Write down a fraction between $\dfrac{7}{12}$ and $\dfrac{4}{7}$.

13 Equivalent fractions and ordering fractions

 **Do not use a calculator**

1 Write down five fractions equal to $\frac{2}{7}$.

2 In this set of fractions there are two families of equal fractions and an odd one out. Find each family and the odd one out.

$\frac{15}{18}$ $\quad$ $\frac{24}{30}$ $\quad$ $\frac{12}{20}$ $\quad$ $\frac{3}{5}$ $\quad$ $\frac{50}{60}$ $\quad$ $\frac{21}{35}$

$\frac{15}{25}$ $\quad$ $\frac{45}{54}$ $\quad$ $\frac{100}{120}$ $\quad$ $\frac{20}{24}$ $\quad$ $\frac{60}{100}$ $\quad$ $\frac{60}{72}$

3 Write each of these times as fractions of 1 day, in their simplest form.

(a) 6 hours $\qquad$ (b) 18 hours

(c) 15 hours $\qquad$ (d) 10 hours

4 Two containers have capacities of 3 litres and 450 ml. What fraction of the larger capacity is the smaller capacity?

5 (a) What fraction of a turn is 135°?

(b) How long does it take the hour hand on a clock to rotate through $\frac{5}{6}$ of a right angle?

6 Put one of the signs <, = > between each pair of fractions to make a correct statement.

(a) $\frac{1}{4}$ and $\frac{1}{3}$ $\quad$ (b) $\frac{2}{7}$ and $\frac{3}{10}$ $\quad$ (c) $\frac{3}{8}$ and $\frac{7}{16}$

(d) $\frac{4}{6}$ and $\frac{18}{27}$ $\quad$ (e) $\frac{5}{6}$ and $\frac{6}{8}$ $\quad$ (f) $\frac{2}{3}$ and $\frac{3}{5}$

(g) $\frac{9}{12}$ and $\frac{21}{28}$ $\quad$ (h) $\frac{4}{6}$ and $\frac{7}{9}$ $\quad$ (i) $\frac{6}{11}$ and $\frac{3}{5}$

7 Write these fractions in order, starting with the smallest:

$\frac{1}{7}$ $\quad$ $\frac{2}{7}$ $\quad$ $\frac{2}{8}$ $\quad$ $\frac{3}{8}$ $\quad$ $\frac{3}{9}$ $\quad$ $\frac{4}{9}$

8 Write each of these sets of fractions in order, starting with the smallest.

(a) $\frac{5}{16}$ $\quad$ $\frac{1}{4}$ $\quad$ $\frac{3}{8}$ $\quad$ (b) $\frac{7}{8}$ $\quad$ $\frac{9}{10}$ $\quad$ $\frac{4}{5}$ $\quad$ (c) $\frac{1}{3}$ $\quad$ $\frac{3}{10}$ $\quad$ $\frac{2}{7}$

9 (a) Which is larger $\frac{4}{5}$ or $\frac{5}{6}$?

(b) Find a fraction which is between $\frac{4}{5}$ and $\frac{5}{6}$.

10 Find a fraction which is between $\frac{1}{100}$ and $\frac{1}{101}$.

14 Using and ordering decimals

LESSON OBJECTIVES

- Understand and use decimal notation
- Order decimals

WORKING INTERACTIVELY

- Ask students what number is half way between 7 and 8. Give the answer as a decimal. (7.5)

- What number is half way between 13 and 14? (13.5)
  Between 40 and 50? (45)
  Between 3.4 and 3.5? (3.45)
  Between 4.2 and 4.6? (4.4)
  Between 6.9 and 7.3? (7.1)
  Ask students for their own suggestions.

- Reverse this. Give two numbers that 13.5 is half way between. (e.g. 13 and 14)

  Give two numbers that 7.35 is half way between. (e.g. 7.3 and 7.4, or 7.34 and 7.36)

  That 9.1 is half way between. (e.g. 9.0 and 9.2, or 8.8 and 9.4, etc.)

  That 19.9 is half way between. (e.g. 19.8 and 20)

- Now draw this number line on the board.

  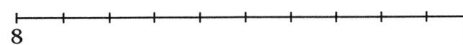

  Get students to help you complete it, so that it looks like this.

  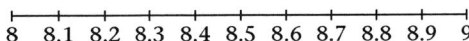

  Change the end points to 4 and 6.
  (4.2, 4.4, 4.6, 4.8, 5, 5.2, 5.4, 5.6, 5.8)

  Change the end points to 3.4 and 3.5.
  (3.41, 3.42, 3.43, 3.44, 3.45, 3.46, 3.47, 3.48, 3.49)

  Change the end points to 6.2 and 6.4.
  (6.22, 6.24, 6.26, 6.28, 6.3, 6.32, 6.34, 6.36, 6.38)

  Change the end points to 9.8 and 10.
  (9.82, 9.84, 9.86, 9.88, 9.9, 9.92, 9.94, 9.96, 9.98)

- Now draw this number line on the board and get students to complete it. (5.25, 5.5, 5.75)

  ```
  ├──┼──┼──┼──┤
  5        6
  ```

  Change the end points to 6 and 8.
  (6.5, 7, 7.5)

  Change the end points to 3.2 and 3.4.
  (3.25, 3.3, 3.35)

  Change the end points to 4.0 and 4.1.
  (4.025, 4.05, 4.075)

- Now start at 7 and get students to count on together in 0.1s. (7.1, 7.2, …, 7.9, 8, etc.)

  Start at 29.5 and count on in 0.1s.
  (29.6, 29.7, 29.8, 29.9, 30, 30.1, …)

  Start at 42 and count on in 0.2s.
  (42, 42.2, 42.4, 42.6, 42.8, 43, 43.2, …)

  Start at 68 and count on in 0.5s.
  (68.5, 69, 69.5, 70, 70.5, …)

  Start at 17 and count on in 0.4s
  (17.4, 17.8, 18.2, 18.6, 19, 19.4, 19.8, 20.2, …)

  Start at 3.6 and count on in 0.01s.
  (3.61, 3.62, 3.63, 3.64, 3.65, 3.66, 3.67, 3.68, 3.69, 3.7, …)

  Start at 8.85 and count on in 0.01s.
  (8.86, 8.87, 8.88, 8.89, 8.9, …)

  Start at 7 and count on in 0.02s.
  (7.02, 7.04, 7.06, 7.08, 7.1, 7.12, …)

  Start at 9.9 and count on in 0.02s.
  (9.92, 9.94, 9.96, 9.98, 10, 10.02, …)

- Now start at 5 and get students to count back together in 0.1s. (4.9, 4.8, 4.7, …)

  Start at 20.5 and count back in 0.1s.
  (20.4, 20.3, 20.2, 20.1, 20, 19.9, …)

  Start at 6 and count back in 0.01s.
  (5.99, 5.98, 5.97, …)

- Take 0.1 off: 6.8, 8, 10, 100 (6.7; 7.9; 9.9; 99.9)
  Take 0.01 off: 4.36, 4.7, 5, 10 (4.35; 4.69; 4.99; 9.99)
  Add 0.01 to: 6.3, 7.9, 4.09 (6.31; 7.91; 4.1)

- How many tens is: 50, 80, 30?   (5, 8, 3)

  How many tens is: 230, 470, 1000?   (23, 47, 100)

  How many tenths is: 0.6, 0.3, 0.1?   (6, 3, 1)

  How many hundredths is:
  0.04, 0.09, 0.16, 0.35?   (4, 9, 16, 35)

  How many tenths is:
  6.4, 3.8, 13.2, 7, 10?   (64, 38, 132, 70, 100)

  How many hundredths is:
  1.23, 1.85, 2.64, 3.5, 7?   (123, 185, 264, 350, 700)

  How many tens is: 35, 65, 278?   (3.5, 6.5, 27.8)

  How many tenths is:
  0.65, 0.34, 0.72, 1.48?   (6.5, 3.4, 7.2, 14.8)

- *Ordering decimals*

  Which is bigger: 6.8 or 6.11?   (6.8)

          5.98 or 6.01?   (6.01)

          0.35 or 0.329?   (0.35)

          10.01 or 7.97?   (10.01)

  You decide which is bigger by comparing the two numbers 'from the left'. The same applies if you have several numbers:

      4.85, 4.839, 4.8099. 0.9989, 4.089

      (0.9989, 4.089, 4.8099, 4.839, 4.85)

INDIVIDUAL WORK

Students work through the classwork sheet.

Review

Mark classwork and review key strategies.

ANSWERS TO THE CLASSWORK SHEET

1 (a) 45   (b) 12.5   (c) 29.5   (d) 6.3   (e) 8.25
    (f) 4.35   (g) 9.95   (h) 2.88

2 (a) (i) 3.5   (ii) 30   (iii) 18.1   (iv) 6.48
    (b) (i) 3.41   (ii) 29.91   (iii) 18.01   (iv) 3.98
    (c) (i) 7.4   (ii) 10.9   (iii) 99.9   (iv) 6.39
    (d) (i) 3.41   (ii) 4.59   (iii) 6.99   (iv) 19.99

3 (a) (i) 5   (ii) 9   (iii) 12
    (b) (i) 40   (ii) 16   (iii) 78
    (c) (i) 35   (ii) 80   (iii) 200
    (d) (i) 236   (ii) 430   (iii) 800

4 (a) 0.3, 0.4, 0.5, 0.9   (b) 0.11, 0.13, 0.7, 0.9
    (c) 6.045, 6.08, 6.1, 6.42
    (d) 0.009 99, 0.0991, 0.101 09, 0.909

HOMEWORK

Page
46

HOMEWORK ANSWERS

Page
134

14 Using and ordering decimals

 Do not use a calculator

1 Write down the number that is half way between
  (a) 40 and 50   (b) 12 and 13   (c) 29 and 30   (d) 6.1 and 6.5
  (e) 8 and 8.5   (f) 4.3 and 4.4   (g) 9.9 and 10   (h) 2.86 and 2.9

2 (a) Add 0.1 to
       (i) 3.4   (ii) 29.9   (iii) 18   (iv) 6.38
   (b) Add 0.01 to
       (i) 3.4   (ii) 29.9   (iii) 18   (iv) 6.38
   (c) Subtract 0.1 from
       (i) 7.5   (ii) 11   (iii) 100   (iv) 4.08
   (d) Subtract 0.01 from
       (i) 3.42   (ii) 4.6   (iii) 7   (iv) 20

3 (a) How many tenths are there in
       (i) 0.5?   (ii) 0.9?   (iii) 1.2?
   (b) How many hundredths are there in
       (i) 0.4?   (ii) 0.16?   (iii) 0.78?
   (c) How many tenths are there in
       (i) 3.5?   (ii) 8?   (iii) 20?
   (d) How many hundredths are there in
       (i) 2.36?   (ii) 4.3?   (iii) 8?

4 Write each set of decimals in order of size, starting with the smallest.
   (a) 0.5, 0.3, 0.4, 0.9   (b) 0.13, 0.11, 0.9, 0.7
   (c) 6.045, 6.1, 6.42, 6.08   (d) 0.909, 0.0991, 0.009 99, 0.101 09

14 Using and ordering decimals

 Do not use a calculator

1 Write down the number that is half way between

(a) 100 and 200   (b) 8 and 9
(c) 99 and 100   (d) 2.3 and 2.4
(e) 6.2 and 7   (f) 5.5 and 5.6
(g) 5.9 and 6   (h) 3.7 and 4

2 (a) Add 0.2 to
(i) 8.7 (ii) 7.8 (iii) 43 (iv) 19.9
(b) Add 0.03 to
(i) 7 (ii) 5.97 (iii) 3.99 (iv) 4.03
(c) Subtract 0.1 from
(i) 5.9 (ii) 8 (iii) 10 (iv) 3.75
(d) Subtract 0.02 from
(i) 4.3 (ii) 2.1 (iii) 9 (iv) 5.01

3 (a) How many tenths are there in
(i) 0.4? (ii) 0.1? (iii) 2.3?
(b) How many hundredths are there in
(i) 0.09? (ii) 0.91? (iii) 0.8?
(c) How many tenths are there in
(i) 7.3? (ii) 6? (iii) 50?
(d) How many hundredths are there in
(i) 5.43? (ii) 6.2? (iii) 10?

4 (a) How many pence are there in
(i) £2.36? (ii) £4.50? (iii) £20?
(b) How many centimetres are there in
(i) 2 m? (ii) 2.3 m?
(iii) 1.78 m?
(c) How many grams are there in
(i) 3 kg? (ii) 4.328 kg?
(iii) 0.6 kg?
(d) How many metres is
(i) 400 cm? (ii) 253 cm?
(iii) 20 cm?

5 Write each set of decimals in order of size, starting with the smallest.
(a) 6.3   6.9   5.8   5.5
(b) 0.4   0.8   0.12   0.16
(c) 5.73   57.2   5.699   5.729
(d) 0.101   0.11   0.0101   1.1001

Lessons in Numeracy (Intermediate) © Longman (an imprint of Pearson Education) 2001

15 Equivalence of fractions and decimals 1

LESSON OBJECTIVES

● Recognise that each terminating decimal is a fraction
● Recognise elementary equivalences between fractions and decimals

WORKING INTERACTIVELY

● Mark this line out in 0.1s, building on the last lesson.

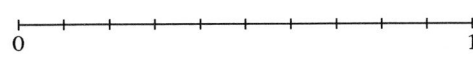

Each of the divisions is $\frac{1}{10}$ (there are 10 of them and $0.1 = \frac{1}{10}$).

● Amend the line to emphasise fifths.

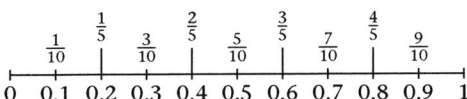

● Use the line to note, for example, that:

$$\frac{1}{2} = \frac{5}{10} = 0.5$$

$$\frac{2}{5} = \frac{4}{10} = 0.4$$

$$0.7 = \frac{7}{10}$$

$$0.8 = \frac{8}{10} = \frac{4}{5}$$

● Build up this line in the same way.

```
        1/4   1/2   3/4
 |---|---|---|---|
 0  0.25 0.5 0.75  1
```

Note that $\frac{1}{4} = 0.25 = \frac{25}{100}$

● Build this line (which can be done by marking mid-points on the previous line).

```
     1/8  1/4  3/8  1/2  5/8  3/4  7/8
 |---|---|---|---|---|---|---|---|
 0 0.125   0.375   0.625   0.875  1
        0.25    0.5    0.75
```

● Point out that, for example, $0.375 = \frac{375}{1000} = \frac{75}{200} = \frac{15}{40} = \frac{3}{8}$

We can use this method for more awkward numbers:

e.g. $0.37 = \frac{37}{100}$

$0.38 = \frac{38}{100} = \frac{19}{50}$

$0.05 = \frac{5}{100} = \frac{1}{20}$

● Neither fractions nor decimals have to be less than 1.

e.g. $3.2 = 3\frac{1}{5}$

$5.25 = 5\frac{1}{4}$

$8.7 = 8\frac{7}{10}$

● So you turn a **decimal** into a **fraction** by putting the correct number of zeros in the denominator and cancelling down.

INDIVIDUAL WORK

Students work through *Part 1* of the classwork sheet.

WORKING INTERACTIVELY

● How do you turn fractions into decimals?
● We shall look at particular examples in this lesson, and consider a general method in lesson 16.
● How do you turn $\frac{3}{20}$ into a decimal? $\frac{3}{20} = \frac{15}{100} = 0.15$
● This is similar: $\frac{123}{500} = \frac{246}{1000} = 0.246$
● What about $\frac{9}{16}$?

One way of dealing with this is to use the fact that $\frac{9}{16}$ is half way between $\frac{1}{2}$ and $\frac{5}{8}$, or 0.5 and 0.625.

So $\frac{9}{16} = 0.5625$

INDIVIDUAL WORK

Students work through the rest of the classwork sheet.

Review

Mark classwork and review key strategies.

- It is worth knowing decimal equivalents of $\frac{1}{4}$s, $\frac{1}{5}$s, $\frac{1}{3}$s and probably $\frac{1}{8}$s.

- To turn a decimal into a fraction, put it over the right number of zeros.

  e.g. $0.3 = \frac{3}{10}$, $0.31 = \frac{31}{100}$, $0.317 = \frac{317}{1000}$

  The fraction can often be cancelled down.

  e.g. $0.36 = \frac{36}{100} = \frac{9}{25}$, $0.35 = \frac{35}{100} = \frac{7}{20}$

  Note that it is much harder to turn a recurring decimal into an exact fraction.

- To turn some fractions into decimals, multiply numerator and denominator by a suitable number so that the denominator becomes a power of 10.

  For example, $\frac{21}{125} = \frac{168}{1000} = 0.168$

ANSWERS TO THE CLASSWORK SHEET

Part 1

1 (a) $3\frac{3}{4}$ (b) $\frac{2}{5}$ (c) $4\frac{4}{5}$ (d) $7\frac{1}{10}$

(e) $4\frac{1}{100}$ (f) $2\frac{5}{8}$ (g) $1\frac{3}{5}$ (h) $12\frac{4}{5}$

(i) $\frac{37}{100}$ (j) $\frac{21}{25}$ (k) $9\frac{999}{1000}$ (l) $\frac{7}{10\,000}$

2 (a) $\frac{1}{20}$, $\frac{3}{10}$, $\frac{1}{4}$, $\frac{7}{20}$, $\frac{9}{20}$, $\frac{11}{20}$, $\frac{13}{20}$, $\frac{3}{4}$, $\frac{17}{20}$, $\frac{19}{20}$

(b) $\frac{3}{50}$, $\frac{4}{25}$, $\frac{13}{50}$, $\frac{9}{25}$, $\frac{23}{50}$, $\frac{14}{25}$, $\frac{33}{50}$, $\frac{19}{25}$, $\frac{43}{50}$, $\frac{24}{25}$

Part 2

1 (a) 2.125 (b) 3.25 (c) 12.6 (d) 0.35
(e) 1.4375 (f) 13.36

2 (a) 0.2 (b) 0.07 (c) 0.08 (d) 0.055
(e) 0.746 (f) 0.925

3 (a) 0.125, 0.375, 0.625, 0.875
(b) 0.0625, 0.1875, 0.3125, 0.4375, 0.5625, 0.6875, 0.8125, 0.9375

HOMEWORK

Page
50

HOMEWORK
ANSWERS
Page
134

Lessons in Numeracy (Intermediate) © Longman (an imprint of **Pearson Education**) 2001

15 Equivalence of fractions and decimals 1

Do not use a calculator

Part 1

1. Write these decimals as fractions in their simplest form.

   (a) 3.75   (b) 0.4   (c) 4.8   (d) 7.1

   (e) 4.01   (f) 2.625   (g) 1.6   (h) 12.8

   (i) 0.37   (j) 0.84   (k) 9.999   (l) 0.0007

2. Write these decimals as fractions in their simplest form.

   (a) 0.05   0.15   0.25   0.35   0.45   0.55   0.65   0.75   0.85   0.95

   (b) 0.06   0.16   0.26   0.36   0.46   0.56   0.66   0.76   0.86   0.96

Part 2

1. Write these fractions as decimals.

   (a) $2\frac{1}{8}$ (b) $3\frac{1}{4}$ (c) $12\frac{3}{5}$ (d) $\frac{7}{20}$ (e) $1\frac{7}{16}$ (f) $13\frac{9}{25}$

2. Write these fractions as decimals.

   (a) $\frac{1}{5}$ (b) $\frac{7}{100}$ (c) $\frac{2}{25}$ (d) $\frac{11}{200}$ (e) $\frac{373}{500}$ (f) $\frac{37}{40}$

3. Write these fractions as decimals.

   (a) $\frac{1}{8}$ $\frac{3}{8}$ $\frac{5}{8}$ $\frac{7}{8}$

   (b) $\frac{1}{16}$ $\frac{3}{16}$ $\frac{5}{16}$ $\frac{7}{16}$ $\frac{9}{16}$ $\frac{11}{16}$ $\frac{13}{16}$ $\frac{15}{16}$

INTERMEDIATE ● CLASSWORK

15 Equivalence of fractions and decimals 1

Do not use a calculator

Part 1

1. Write these decimals as fractions in their simplest form.

   (a) 3.75 (b) 0.4 (c) 4.8 (d) 7.1

   (e) 4.01 (f) 2.625 (g) 1.6 (h) 12.8

   (i) 0.37 (j) 0.84 (k) 9.999 (l) 0.0007

2. Write these decimals as fractions in their simplest form.

   (a) 0.05 0.15 0.25 0.35 0.45 0.55 0.65 0.75 0.85 0.95

   (b) 0.06 0.16 0.26 0.36 0.46 0.56 0.66 0.76 0.86 0.96

Part 2

1. Write these fractions as decimals.

   (a) $2\frac{1}{8}$ (b) $3\frac{1}{4}$ (c) $12\frac{3}{5}$ (d) $\frac{7}{20}$ (e) $1\frac{7}{16}$ (f) $13\frac{9}{25}$

2. Write these fractions as decimals.

   (a) $\frac{1}{5}$ (b) $\frac{7}{100}$ (c) $\frac{2}{25}$ (d) $\frac{11}{200}$ (e) $\frac{373}{500}$ (f) $\frac{37}{40}$

3. Write these fractions as decimals.

   (a) $\frac{1}{8}$ $\frac{3}{8}$ $\frac{5}{8}$ $\frac{7}{8}$

   (b) $\frac{1}{16}$ $\frac{3}{16}$ $\frac{5}{16}$ $\frac{7}{16}$ $\frac{9}{16}$ $\frac{11}{16}$ $\frac{13}{16}$ $\frac{15}{16}$

Lessons in Numeracy (Intermediate) © Longman (an imprint of Pearson Education) 2001

15 Equivalence of fractions and decimals 1

Do not use a calculator

1 Write these fractions as decimals.

(a) $\frac{2}{5}$ (b) $\frac{37}{100}$ (c) $\frac{3}{20}$ (d) $\frac{9}{100}$ (e) $\frac{1}{1000}$

2 Write these numbers as decimals.

(a) $\frac{11}{5}$ (b) $3\frac{3}{4}$ (c) $8\frac{7}{10}$ (d) $\frac{1}{8}$

(e) $4\frac{3}{8}$ (f) $7\frac{11}{50}$ (g) $2\frac{13}{20}$ (h) $6\frac{13}{16}$

3 (a) Change these fractions to decimals.

$\frac{3}{5}$ $\frac{5}{8}$ $\frac{4}{5}$ $\frac{1}{2}$ $\frac{3}{4}$

(b) List the fractions in order of size.

4 Write each of these numbers as a fraction in its simplest form.

(a) 0.4   (b) 0.8   (c) 2.25   (d) 3.15   (e) 4.56

(f) 0.125   (g) 7.625   (h) 0.003   (i) 0.008

5 Write each of these numbers as a fraction in its simplest form.

(a) 0.04   (b) 0.14   (c) 0.24   (d) 0.34   (e) 0.44

(f) 0.54   (g) 0.64   (h) 0.74   (i) 0.84

Lessons in Numeracy (Intermediate) © Longman (an imprint of Pearson Education) 2001

INTERMEDIATE ● HOMEWORK

15 Equivalence of fractions and decimals 1

Do not use a calculator

1 Write these fractions as decimals.

(a) $\frac{2}{5}$ (b) $\frac{37}{100}$ (c) $\frac{3}{20}$ (d) $\frac{9}{100}$ (e) $\frac{1}{1000}$

2 Write these numbers as decimals.

(a) $\frac{11}{5}$ (b) $3\frac{3}{4}$ (c) $8\frac{7}{10}$ (d) $\frac{1}{8}$

(e) $4\frac{3}{8}$ (f) $7\frac{11}{50}$ (g) $2\frac{13}{20}$ (h) $6\frac{13}{16}$

3 (a) Change these fractions to decimals.

$\frac{3}{5}$ $\frac{5}{8}$ $\frac{4}{5}$ $\frac{1}{2}$ $\frac{3}{4}$

(b) List the fractions in order of size.

4 Write each of these numbers as a fraction in its simplest form.

(a) 0.4   (b) 0.8   (c) 2.25   (d) 3.15   (e) 4.56

(f) 0.125   (g) 7.625   (h) 0.003   (i) 0.008

5 Write each of these numbers as a fraction in its simplest form.

(a) 0.04   (b) 0.14   (c) 0.24   (d) 0.34   (e) 0.44

(f) 0.54   (g) 0.64   (h) 0.74   (i) 0.84

Lessons in Numeracy (Intermediate) © Longman (an imprint of Pearson Education) 2001

16 Equivalence of fractions and decimals 2

> ## LESSON OBJECTIVES
> - Perform short division to convert a fraction to a decimal
> - Recognise that recurring decimals are exact fractions
> - Recognise that some exact fractions are recurring decimals
> - Distinguish between fractions which are represented by terminating decimals (denominators that have only prime factors 2 and 5) and other fractions which are represented by recurring decimals

WORKING INTERACTIVELY

- We've changed $\frac{1}{5}$s, $\frac{1}{4}$s, $\frac{1}{8}$s into decimals.

  What about $\frac{1}{3}$s?

  Remember that $\frac{1}{3}$ means $1 \div 3$ and so you do the division.

  Do the division on the board and discuss the notion that it goes on for ever – recurring.

  Repeat for $\frac{2}{3}$

  Introduce dot notation: $\frac{1}{3} = 0.3333 \ldots = 0.\dot{3}$

  $\frac{2}{3} = 0.6666 \ldots = 0.\dot{6}$

- Now show students how to obtain sixths as recurring decimals.

  Remember that $\frac{1}{6}$ means $1 \div 6$.

  Do the division on the board and again point out that it goes on for ever – recurring.

  Repeat for $\frac{5}{6}$.

  Write using dot notation: $\frac{1}{6} = 0.1666 \ldots = 0.1\dot{6}$

  $\frac{5}{6} = 0.8333 \ldots = 0.8\dot{3}$

  Obtain $\frac{1}{7}, \frac{2}{7}, \frac{3}{7}, \frac{4}{7}, \frac{5}{7}, \frac{6}{7}$ as recurring decimals by division (or by using a calculator for some of it, if you prefer).

  A wheel can be used to summarise the results for sevenths.

  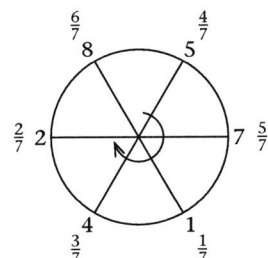

- Turn $\frac{7}{40}$ into a decimal by using short division
  ($= 0.175$). This does *not* recur.

INDIVIDUAL WORK

Which fractions recur and which do not?

Students work through the classwork sheet, which aims to get them to discover which fractions recur and which do not. Decide whether you want students to do this work with or without a calculator. They should work at least some of the sheet without a calculator, so that they practise changing a fraction to a decimal using short division.

Review

Mark classwork and discuss with students the answer to the question: which fractions recur? Students will have divided the fractions into two lists: those that recur and those that do not and will have factorised the denominators.

- They need to observe that *when fractions are written in their lowest terms*, the denominators of fractions that terminate only have prime factors of 2 and 5 in their factorisation.

- This is because any terminating decimal written as a fraction has a denominator of the form $10^n = 2^n \times 5^n$. So, even when this fraction is cancelled down, the only prime factors that can appear in the denominator are 2 and 5.

- Of course, other factors can be introduced into the denominator by multiplying top and bottom by the same number. But then the fraction is not in its lowest terms.

ANSWERS TO THE CLASSWORK SHEET

1 (a) 0.6̇; recurs   (b) 0.25   (c) 0.6
   (d) 0.83̇; recurs   (e) 0.5̇71 428̇; recurs   (f) 0.625
   (g) 0.4̇; recurs   (h) 0.7   (i) 0.8̇1̇; recurs
   (j) 0.583̇; recurs

2 (a) 0.3̇07 629̇; recurs   (b) 0.3125   (c) 0.32
   (d) 0.23̇; recurs   (e) 0.325   (f) 0.94
   (g) 0.2̇68 29̇; recurs   (h) 0.94̇; recurs

3

Terminating decimals	Denominator as product of prime factors	Recurring decimals	Denominator as product of prime factors
$\frac{1}{4}$	2 × 2	$\frac{2}{3}$	3
$\frac{3}{5}$	5	$\frac{5}{6}$	2 × 3
$\frac{5}{8}$	2 × 2 × 2	$\frac{4}{7}$	7
$\frac{7}{10}$	2 × 5	$\frac{4}{9}$	3 × 3
$\frac{5}{16}$	2 × 2 × 2 × 2	$\frac{9}{11}$	11
$\frac{8}{25}$	5 × 5	$\frac{7}{12}$	2 × 2 × 3
$\frac{13}{40}$	2 × 2 × 2 × 5	$\frac{4}{13}$	13
$\frac{47}{50}$	2 × 5 × 5	$\frac{7}{30}$	2 × 3 × 5
		$\frac{11}{41}$	41
		$\frac{17}{18}$	2 × 3 × 3

4 Terminates when denominator only has prime factors of 2 and/or 5. Otherwise recurs. (But fractions have to be in their simplest form before this rule can be applied: see question 5.)

5 (a) $\frac{9}{12} = 0.75$; terminates because $\frac{9}{12} = \frac{3}{4} = \frac{3}{(2 \times 2)}$

   (b) $\frac{15}{24} = 0.625$; terminates because $\frac{15}{24} = \frac{5}{8} = \frac{5}{(2 \times 2 \times 2)}$

   (c) $\frac{21}{35} = 0.6$; terminates because $\frac{21}{35} = \frac{3}{5}$

HOMEWORK

Page 59

HOMEWORK ANSWERS

Page 135

Equivalence of fractions and decimals 2

 Do not use a calculator for question 1

1 Write each of these fractions as a decimal and decide whether it terminates or recurs.

(a) $\frac{2}{3}$ (b) $\frac{1}{4}$ (c) $\frac{3}{5}$ (d) $\frac{5}{6}$ (e) $\frac{4}{7}$ (f) $\frac{5}{8}$ (g) $\frac{4}{9}$ (h) $\frac{7}{10}$ (i) $\frac{9}{11}$ (j) $\frac{7}{12}$

You may use a calculator for questions 2 to 5

2 Write each of these fractions as a decimal and decide whether it terminates or recurs.

(a) $\frac{4}{13}$ (b) $\frac{5}{16}$ (c) $\frac{8}{25}$ (d) $\frac{7}{30}$ (e) $\frac{13}{40}$ (f) $\frac{47}{50}$ (g) $\frac{11}{41}$ (h) $\frac{17}{18}$

3 Copy this table. Using your answers to questions 1 and 2, decide where each of the fractions belongs. Complete the columns for products of prime factors.

Terminating decimals	Denominator as product of prime factors	Recurring decimals	Denominator as product of prime factors
$\frac{1}{4}$	2×2	$\frac{2}{3}$	3
		$\frac{5}{6}$	2×3

4 Study the second and fourth columns of your table. Use these to discover a rule for deciding which fractions are terminating decimals and which are recurring decimals.

5 If you have found the rule correctly, you may think these fractions break the rule. Write each of them as a decimal and then work out why the rule is not broken.

(a) $\frac{9}{12}$ (b) $\frac{15}{24}$ (c) $\frac{21}{35}$

16 Equivalence of fractions and decimals 2

Do not use a calculator for questions 1 to 3

You may use a calculator for question 4

1 Write each of these fractions as a decimal, stating clearly whether it terminates or recurs.

(a) $\dfrac{1}{3}$ (b) $\dfrac{3}{4}$ (c) $\dfrac{2}{5}$ (d) $\dfrac{1}{6}$ (e) $\dfrac{3}{7}$

(f) $\dfrac{3}{8}$ (g) $\dfrac{5}{9}$ (h) $\dfrac{3}{10}$ (i) $\dfrac{7}{11}$ (j) $\dfrac{11}{12}$

2 There is a rule for deciding which fraction are terminating decimals and which are recurring decimals.

Use this rule to decide which of these fractions are recurring decimals. (You do not need to write the fractions as decimals.)

(a) $\dfrac{7}{8}$ (b) $\dfrac{10}{11}$ (c) $\dfrac{6}{16}$ (d) $\dfrac{5}{9}$ (e) $\dfrac{17}{20}$

(f) $\dfrac{33}{80}$ (g) $\dfrac{13}{70}$ (h) $\dfrac{7}{60}$ (i) $\dfrac{137}{200}$ (j) $\dfrac{3}{38}$

3 Decide which of these fractions are terminating decimals and which are recurring decimals. *You need to be careful!* (You do not need to write the fractions as decimals.)

(a) $\dfrac{3}{6}$ (b) $\dfrac{6}{8}$ (c) $\dfrac{10}{12}$

(d) $\dfrac{14}{21}$ (e) $\dfrac{9}{24}$ (f) $\dfrac{21}{70}$

4 This wheel can be used to show how $\dfrac{1}{7}, \dfrac{2}{7}, \dfrac{3}{7}, \dfrac{4}{7}, \dfrac{5}{7}$ and $\dfrac{6}{7}$ are written as recurring decimals.

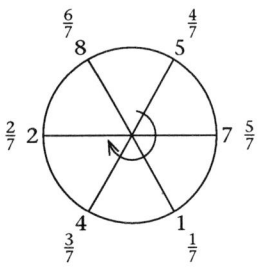

(a) Write $\dfrac{1}{13}, \dfrac{2}{13}, \dfrac{3}{13}, \dfrac{4}{13}, \dfrac{5}{13}, \dfrac{6}{13}, \dfrac{7}{13}, \dfrac{8}{13}, \dfrac{9}{13}, \dfrac{10}{13}, \dfrac{11}{13}, \dfrac{12}{13}$ as recurring decimals.

(b) Summarise your results for 13ths using *two* wheels.

17 Multiplying and dividing decimal numbers

LESSON OBJECTIVES
- Multiply and divide decimal numbers mentally
- Develop a range of strategies for mental calculation

WORKING INTERACTIVELY

- Students need to be clear about how to multiply and divide by powers of 10. They need to understand that the decimal point is a fixed marker, indicating the separation between the units and tenths digits. Multiplication by 10 moves each digit one place to the left; dividing by ten moves each digit one place to the right. Students need to be able to understand and work with this in whatever way works for them. Discuss these examples:

  6.14×10 (61.4)

  $3460 \div 100$ (34.6)

  $48.3 \div 1000$ (0.0483)

  0.7 of 8
  (= 5.6: $7 \times 8 = 56$ and divide by 10, or 0.1 of 8 is 0.8, so 0.7 of 8 is 7×0.8)

  0.3×0.04
  (= 0.012: $3 \times 4 = 12$ and divide by $10 \times 100 = 1000$)

  $24 \div 0.3$
  (= 80: $24 \div 3 = 8$, dividing by a number 10 times smaller gives answer 10 times bigger; or, $24 \div 0.3 = 240 \div 3 = 80$)

  $0.12 \div 0.3$
  (= 0.4 because $0.12 \div 3 = 0.04$; or, $0.12 \div 0.3 = 1.2 \div 3 = 0.4$)

INDIVIDUAL WORK

Students work through the classwork sheet.

HOMEWORK

Page
57

HOMEWORK
ANSWERS
Page
135

Review

Mark any classwork and review strategies:

- To multiply by 10 move the digits one place to the left. Since 100 is 10×10 and 1000 is $10 \times 10 \times 10$ this works for multiplying by 100 and 1000 too.

- To divide by 10 move the digits one place to the right. Dividing by 100 or 1000 work similarly.

- To multiply or divide two decimals, use a combination of known number facts for integers and multiplication or division by 10, 100, 1000, etc.

- When dividing two decimals it might sometimes be useful to know that the answer to the division remains the same if both numbers are multiplied by a power of 10:

  e.g. $4.5 \div 0.9 = 45 \div 9 = 5$

ANSWERS TO THE CLASSWORK SHEET

1 (a) 150 (b) 63.8 (c) 6.8 (d) 0.43 (e) 4500
  (f) 450 (g) 46.7 (h) 8 (i) 14 700 (j) 35

2 (a) 23 (b) 2.8 (c) 3.72 (d) 6.8 (e) 12
  (f) 1.8 (g) 0.45 (h) 0.000 67 (i) 0.32 (j) 0.0068

3 (a) 48 (b) 90 (c) 0.38 (d) 0.79 (e) 0.5
  (f) 0.028 (g) 490 (h) 1000 (i) 100

4 (a) 18 (b) 1.3 (c) 0.28 (d) 0.18 (e) 0.5 (f) 0.2
  (g) 150 (h) 16 (i) 0.2 (j) 0.003 (k) 60 (l) 0.9

5 (a) 0.23 (b) 1.09 (c) 2.86

17 Multiplying and dividing decimal numbers

 **Do not use a calculator**

1 Calculate these.

(a) 15×10 (b) 6.38×10 (c) 0.68×10 (d) 0.043×10 (e) 45×100

(f) 4.5×100 (g) 0.467×100 (h) 0.08×100 (i) 14.7×1000 (j) 0.035×1000

2 Calculate these.

(a) $230 \div 10$ (b) $28 \div 10$ (c) $37.2 \div 10$ (d) $0.68 \div 10$ (e) $1200 \div 100$

(f) $180 \div 100$ (g) $45 \div 100$ (h) $0.067 \div 100$ (i) $320 \div 1000$ (j) $6.8 \div 1000$

3 Copy these, replacing the ? by a number.

(a) $4.8 \times 10 = ?$ (b) $100 \times 0.9 = ?$ (c) $10 \times ? = 3.8$

(d) $100 \times ? = 79$ (e) $5 \div 10 = ?$ (f) $0.28 \div 10 = ?$

(g) $? \div 100 = 4.9$ (h) $0.42 \times ? = 420$ (i) $58 \div ? = 0.58$

4 Calculate these.

(a) 60×0.3 (b) 13×0.1 (c) 1.4×0.2 (d) 0.6×0.3

(e) $0.4 \div 0.8$ (f) $0.12 \div 0.6$ (g) $60 \div 0.4$ (h) $12.8 \div 0.8$

(i) $0.08 \div 0.4$ (j) $0.024 \div 8$ (k) $4.2 \div 0.07$ (l) $0.81 \div 0.9$

5 Calculate these, correct to two decimal places.

(a) $0.7 \div 3$ (b) $1.2 \div 1.1$ (c) $0.2 \div 0.07$

17 Multiplying and dividing numbers

Do not use a calculator

Calculate these.

1 0.2×0.8 **2** 0.02×45 **3** 0.3×35

4 1.3×25 **5** 0.4×0.7 **6** 0.05×460

7 2.4×250 **8** 1.7×500 **9** 600×0.8

10 0.7^2 **11** 1.2^2 **12** 0.08^2

13 2.4^2 **14** 3.8^2 **15** 4.2×5.7

16 $9 \div 2$ **17** $17 \div 4$ **18** $24 \div 0.2$

19 $15 \div 0.3$ **20** $0.9 \div 0.3$ **21** $0.7 \div 0.2$

22 $0.8 \div 4$ **23** $0.8 \div 0.04$ **24** $1.8 \div 0.09$

25 $7.4 \div 4$ **26** $3.84 \div 0.8$ **27** $504 \div 0.07$

Calculate these, correct to 2 decimal places.

28 $4.7 \div 6$ **29** $4.3 \div 0.9$ **30** $0.2 \div 0.7$

Lessons in Numeracy (Intermediate) © Longman (an imprint of Pearson Education) 2001

INTERMEDIATE ● HOMEWORK

17 Multiplying and dividing numbers

Do not use a calculator

Calculate these.

1 0.2×0.8 **2** 0.02×45 **3** 0.3×35

4 1.3×25 **5** 0.4×0.7 **6** 0.05×460

7 2.4×250 **8** 1.7×500 **9** 600×0.8

10 0.7^2 **11** 1.2^2 **12** 0.08^2

13 2.4^2 **14** 3.8^2 **15** 4.2×5.7

16 $9 \div 2$ **17** $17 \div 4$ **18** $24 \div 0.2$

19 $15 \div 0.3$ **20** $0.9 \div 0.3$ **21** $0.7 \div 0.2$

22 $0.8 \div 4$ **23** $0.8 \div 0.04$ **24** $1.8 \div 0.09$

25 $7.4 \div 4$ **26** $3.84 \div 0.8$ **27** $504 \div 0.07$

Calculate these, correct to 2 decimal places.

28 $4.7 \div 6$ **29** $4.3 \div 0.9$ **30** $0.2 \div 0.7$

Lessons in Numeracy (Intermediate) © Longman (an imprint of Pearson Education) 2001

18 The four rules of decimals

LESSON OBJECTIVES

- Add and subtract decimal numbers mentally
- Multiply and divide decimal numbers mentally
- Develop a range of strategies for mental calculation

WORKING INTERACTIVELY

- Revisit ideas of lesson 17 and include a check on addition and, particularly, subtraction of decimal numbers (e.g. 30 − 13.98 = 16.02).

- Discuss methods for more difficult multiplication and division examples
  (e.g. 4.3 × 7.6, 0.27 × 5.6, 5.2 ÷ 0.04, 37.38 ÷ 0.14).

- A sensible starting point is to estimate the answers, where appropriate:

  e.g. $4.3 \times 7.6 \approx 4 \times 8 = 32$

  $0.27 \times 5.6 \approx 0.3 \times 6 = 1.8$

  $5.2 \div 0.04 \approx 5 \div 0.05 = 100$

  $37.38 \div 0.14 \approx 40 \div 0.1 = 400$

- Students can use one of the following methods, or a method they already know.

- Multiplication

  4.3×7.6

  Method 1

  43 × 76 = 3268
  There are 2 digits after the decimal point in the question (having the effect of dividing the product by 100). So there are 2 digits in the answer.

  So the answer is 32.68

  0.27×5.6

  27 × 56 = 1512

  There are 3 digits after the decimal point in the question. So there are 3 digits in the answer.

  So the answer is 1.512

  Method 2

  $4 \quad \times 7.6 = 30.4$

  $\underline{0.3 \times 7.6 = \quad 2.28}$

  $4.3 \times 7.6 = 32.68$

  $0.1 \times 5.6 = 0.56$

  $0.2 \times 5.6 = 1.12$

  $0.01 \times 5.6 = 0.056$

  $0.07 \times 5.6 = \underline{0.392}$

  $0.27 \times 5.6 = 1.512$

- Division

  Method 1

  $5.2 \div 0.04$
  $= 52 \div 0.4$
  $= 520 \div 4$
  $= 130$

  Method 2

  $\qquad\qquad 5.2$
  $\underline{100} \times 0.04 = \underline{-4}$
  $\qquad\qquad 1.2$
  $\underline{10} \times 0.04 = \underline{-0.4}$
  $\qquad\qquad 0.8$
  $\underline{20} \times 0.04 = \underline{-0.8}$
  $\qquad\qquad\quad 0$

  So $5.2 \div 0.04 = 100 + 10 + 20 = 130$

INDIVIDUAL WORK

Students work through the classwork sheet.

Review

Mark any classwork and review strategies. In particular, ensure that students are confident about a method for multiplying and dividing numbers without a calculator.

ANSWERS TO THE CLASSWORK SHEET

1	12.15	**2**	0.024
3	22.001	**4**	26.02
5	7.33	**6**	22.528
7	32.8779	**8**	10.3
9	3.3	**10**	16.1
11	32.5	**12**	23.94
13	14.44	**14**	239.2
15	2.241	**16**	120
17	1.45	**18**	30
19	14.44	**20**	0.29

HOMEWORK

Page
60

HOMEWORK
ANSWERS
Page
135

18 The four rules of decimals

Do not use a calculator

Calculate these.

1 3.45 + 8.7

2 0.064 – 0.04

3 21.83 + 0.171

4 42 – 15.98

5 7.4 – 0.07

6 25.031 – 2.503

7 33.21 – 0.3321

8 4 + 5.6 + 0.7

9 5.6 + 4.5 – 6.8

10 21.2 + 7.8 – 12.9

11 1.3 × 25

12 4.2 × 5.7

13 3.8²

14 0.52 × 460

15 0.27 × 8.3

16 24 ÷ 0.2

17 5.8 ÷ 4

18 4.8 ÷ 0.16

Calculate these, correct to 2 decimal places.

19 13 ÷ 0.9

20 0.2 ÷ 0.7

Lessons in Numeracy (Intermediate) © Longman (an imprint of Pearson Education) 2001

INTERMEDIATE ● CLASSWORK

18 The four rules of decimals

Do not use a calculator

Calculate these.

1 3.45 + 8.7

2 0.064 – 0.04

3 21.83 + 0.171

4 42 – 15.98

5 7.4 – 0.07

6 25.031 – 2.503

7 33.21 – 0.3321

8 4 + 5.6 + 0.7

9 5.6 + 4.5 – 6.8

10 21.2 + 7.8 – 12.9

11 1.3 × 25

12 4.2 × 5.7

13 3.8²

14 0.52 × 460

15 0.27 × 8.3

16 24 ÷ 0.2

17 5.8 ÷ 4

18 4.8 ÷ 0.16

Calculate these, correct to 2 decimal places.

19 13 ÷ 0.9

20 0.2 ÷ 0.7

Lessons in Numeracy (Intermediate) © Longman (an imprint of Pearson Education) 2001

18 The four rules of decimals

Do not use a calculator

Calculate these.

1 5.3 + 17.45

2 0.68 + 1.7

3 12 − 1.95

4 1.007 − 0.468

5 123.8 − 67.83

6 4.2 + 9.1 − 7.8

7 5.63 + 0.72 − 0.062

8 49.8 − 0.498

9 0.2 × 45

10 0.003 × 35

11 4 × 25

12 0.4 × 0.7

13 2.1 × 1.9

14 0.38 × 85

15 2.1 × 34.6

16 4.7²

17 17 ÷ 4

18 15 ÷ 0.3

19 0.7 ÷ 0.2

20 8.64 ÷ 3.6

21 0.48 ÷ 160

22 16.38 ÷ 0.26

23 1.2² − 0.8²

24 5.3²

25 0.8 × 6 − 12 × 0.04

26 243.6 ÷ 0.42

Calculate these, correct to 2 decimal places.

27 100 ÷ 0.7

28 0.79 ÷ 1.3

29 14 ÷ 2.7

30 0.29 ÷ 3.2

Lessons in Numeracy (Intermediate) © Longman (an imprint of Pearson Education) 2001

INTERMEDIATE • HOMEWORK

18 The four rules of decimals

Do not use a calculator

Calculate these.

1 5.3 + 17.45

2 0.68 + 1.7

3 12 − 1.95

4 1.007 − 0.468

5 123.8 − 67.83

6 4.2 + 9.1 − 7.8

7 5.63 + 0.72 − 0.062

8 49.8 − 0.498

9 0.2 × 45

10 0.003 × 35

11 4 × 25

12 0.4 × 0.7

13 2.1 × 1.9

14 0.38 × 85

15 2.1 × 34.6

16 4.7²

17 17 ÷ 4

18 15 ÷ 0.3

19 0.7 ÷ 0.2

20 8.64 ÷ 3.6

21 0.48 ÷ 160

22 16.38 ÷ 0.26

23 1.2² − 0.8²

24 5.3²

25 0.8 × 6 − 12 × 0.04

26 243.6 ÷ 0.42

Calculate these, correct to 2 decimal places.

27 100 ÷ 0.7

28 0.79 ÷ 1.3

29 14 ÷ 2.7

30 0.29 ÷ 3.2

Lessons in Numeracy (Intermediate) © Longman (an imprint of Pearson Education) 2001

19 Fractions, decimals and percentages

WORKING INTERACTIVELY

Per cent means 'out of 100' or 'for every 100.'

So, 37% means $\frac{37}{100}$ or 0.37

3% means $\frac{3}{100}$ or 0.03

Explain how you know that

$50\% = \frac{1}{2} = 0.5$ $\qquad 25\% = \frac{1}{4} = 0.25$ $\qquad 20\% = \frac{1}{5} = 0.2$

$15\% = \frac{15}{100} = \frac{3}{20} = 0.15$

$\frac{3}{4} = 75\% = 0.75$ $\qquad \frac{2}{5} = 40\% = 0.4$ $\qquad \frac{1}{3} = 33\frac{1}{3}\% = 0.\dot{3}$

$\frac{1}{8} = \frac{1}{8} \times 100\% = \frac{100}{8}\% = 12.5\%$

Which is bigger: 35% or $\frac{1}{3}$

$\qquad\qquad$ 65% or $\frac{5}{8}$

$\qquad\qquad$ 0.85 or $\frac{4}{5}$?

What is $\frac{3}{20}$ as a percentage?

$\left(\frac{3}{20} = \frac{3}{20} \times 100\% = \frac{300}{20}\% = \frac{30}{2}\% = 15\%\right)$

What is $\frac{3}{8}$ as a percentage?

$\left(\frac{3}{8} = \frac{3}{8} \times 100\% = \frac{300}{8}\% = 37.5\%\right)$

What is $\frac{13}{40}$ as a percentage?

$\left(\frac{13}{40} = \frac{13}{40} \times 100\% = \frac{1300}{40}\% = \frac{130}{4}\% = 32.5\%\right)$

What is 87.5% as a fraction?

$\left(\text{Remember } 12.5\% = \frac{1}{8}, \text{ then } 87.5\% = \frac{7}{8}.\right.$

Alternatively, $87.5\% = \frac{875}{1000} = \frac{7}{8}\Big)$

What is $6\frac{2}{3}\%$ as a fraction?

$\left(6\frac{2}{3}\% = \frac{6\frac{2}{3}}{100} = \frac{20}{300} = \frac{1}{15}\right)$

INDIVIDUAL WORK

Students work through the classwork sheet.

Review

Mark any classwork and review these results, which should be known:

● $\frac{1}{100} = 1\%$ $\quad \frac{1}{10} = 10\%$

● $\frac{1}{2} = 0.5 = 50\%$ $\quad \frac{1}{4} = 0.25 = 25\%$ $\quad \frac{3}{4} = 0.75 = 75\%$

● $\frac{1}{5} = 0.2 = 20\%$, from which students can deduce

$\frac{2}{5} = 40\%$ $\quad \frac{3}{5} = 60\%$ $\quad \frac{4}{5} = 80\%$

● $\frac{1}{8} = 0.125 = 12.5\%$, from which students can deduce

$\frac{3}{8} = 37.5\%$ $\quad \frac{5}{8} = 62.5\%$ $\quad \frac{7}{8} = 87.5\%$

● $\frac{1}{3} = 33\frac{1}{3}\%$ $\quad \frac{2}{3} = 66\frac{2}{3}\%$

● General strategies:

Turning a percentage into a decimal into a fraction:
$37\% = 0.37 = \frac{37}{100}$

Turning a fraction into a decimal into a percentage:
$\frac{3}{40} = 0.075$ (divide 3 by 40 as in lesson 15) $= 7.5\%$

or $\quad \frac{3}{40} = \frac{3}{40} \times 100\% = \frac{300}{40}\% = \frac{30}{4}\% = 7.5\%$

ANSWERS TO THE CLASSWORK SHEET

1 (a) 0.13 (b) 0.63 (c) 0.07 (d) 0.01 (e) 0.002

2 (a) $\frac{1}{4}$ (b) $\frac{2}{5}$ (c) $\frac{1}{10}$ (d) $\frac{1}{20}$ (e) $\frac{2}{25}$

3 (a) 52% (b) 90% (c) 35% (d) 17.5%

4

Fraction	Decimal	Percentage
$\frac{2}{5}$	0.4	40%
$\frac{3}{4}$	0.75	75%
$\frac{7}{10}$	0.7	70%
$\frac{2}{3}$	0.\dot{6}	$66\frac{2}{3}\%$
$\frac{1}{4}$	0.25	25%
$\frac{3}{20}$	0.15	15%

5 $0.3 = \frac{3}{10}, \frac{4}{5} = 0.8 = 80\%, 35\% = \frac{7}{20} = 0.35, 5\% = \frac{1}{20}, 20\% = \frac{1}{5},$

$0.28 = 28\% = \frac{7}{25}$ (8%, 70% and 3% have no equivalents)

6 $14\% = 0.14, \frac{1}{5} = 0.2, 0.21, 22\% = 0.22, \frac{2}{9} = 0.\dot{2}, \frac{1}{4} = 0.25,$

$\frac{21}{80} = 0.2625$

7 $\frac{7}{11} = 0.\dot{6}\dot{3}$. Smaller: 0.6, $\frac{5}{8}$ ($= 0.625$), $63\frac{1}{2}\%$ ($= 0.635$)

19 Fractions, decimals and percentages

Do not use a calculator

1 Write these percentages as decimals.

(a) 13%   (b) 63%   (c) 7%   (d) 1%   (e) 0.2%

2 Convert these percentages to fractions in their simplest form.

(a) 25%   (b) 40%   (c) 10%   (d) 5%   (e) 8%

3 Convert these fractions to percentages.

(a) $\frac{13}{25}$ (b) $\frac{9}{10}$ (c) $\frac{7}{20}$ (d) $\frac{7}{40}$

4 Copy and complete this table.

Fraction	Decimal	Percentage
$\frac{2}{5}$	0.4	40%
	0.75	
		70%
$\frac{2}{3}$		
$\frac{1}{4}$		
		15%

5 Some of these fractions, decimals and percentages are equivalent. Find them.

0.3 $\frac{4}{5}$ 35%   20%   5%   0.28 $\frac{3}{10}$ 28% $\frac{7}{20}$

0.35 $\frac{7}{25}$ 0.8   3% $\frac{1}{5}$ $\frac{1}{20}$ 8%   70%   80%

6 Arrange these numbers in order of size, starting with the smallest.

22% $\frac{2}{9}$ 0.29 $\frac{1}{4}$ 14%   0.21 $\frac{21}{80}$ $\frac{1}{5}$

7 Which of these numbers is less than $\frac{7}{11}$?

$\frac{2}{3}$ 0.6   65% $\frac{5}{8}$ $63\frac{1}{2}$%   0.64

Lessons in Numeracy (Intermediate) © Longman (an imprint of Pearson Education) 2001

Fractions, decimals and percentages

 **Do not use a calculator for questions 1 to 7**

1 Write these percentages as decimals.
(a) 17% (b) 78% (c) 6% (d) 0.3%

2 Convert these percentages to fractions in their simplest form.
(a) 75% (b) 80% (c) 6% (d) 0.5%

3 Convert these fractions to percentages.
(a) $\frac{37}{50}$ (b) $\frac{7}{10}$ (c) $\frac{13}{20}$ (d) $\frac{9}{40}$

4 Copy and complete this table.

Fraction	Decimal	Percentage
$\frac{4}{5}$		
$\frac{1}{3}$		
	0.45	
	0.125	
		24%
		8%

5 Three students took a General Knowledge test.
Sean scored $\frac{2}{3}$ of the total marks.
Shardi scored 65%.
Tracey scored $\frac{3}{5}$ of the total marks.
Who scored the highest marks? Show all your working.

6 In the Fizzy Fitness sports club $\frac{2}{5}$ of the membership is female.
In the Endless Exercise sports club 65% of the members are male.
In the Wacky Workout sports club there are 5 men for every 3 women.
Which sports club has the highest proportion of women? Show all your working.

7 Write each of these percentages as a decimal and as a fraction.
(a) $37\frac{1}{2}\%$ (b) $3\frac{1}{2}\%$ (c) $16\frac{2}{3}\%$

You may use a calculator for questions 8 and 9

8 Arrange these numbers in order of size, starting with the smallest.
$2\frac{2}{7}$ $\frac{2}{7}$ 0.227   77% $\frac{7}{27}$
$\frac{7}{22}$ 22%   27%   2.7 $\frac{22}{7}$

9 Write each of these fractions as percentages, correct to the nearest per cent, and then arrange the fractions in order of size.
$\frac{5}{13}$ $\frac{8}{17}$ $\frac{11}{24}$ $\frac{11}{27}$ $\frac{13}{31}$ $\frac{25}{52}$

20 Finding percentages without a calculator

LESSON OBJECTIVES

● Understand that 'percentage' means 'number of parts per 100' and 'so many hundredths of'

● Solve percentage problems, including percentage increase and decrease

WORKING INTERACTIVELY

● Remind students that 3% means 0.03 or $\frac{3}{100}$ and 42% means 0.42 or $\frac{42}{100}$.

So, 3% of 6 means $\frac{3}{100}$ of 6 = 0.18 and

42% of 6 means $\frac{42}{100}$ of 6 = 2.52.

● How would you work these out?

15% of 6 (= 0.9)   8% of 6 (= 0.48)

32% of 6 (= 1.92)

Discuss quick techniques for calculating percentages:
For example, what is 15% of 45?

10% of 45   = 4.5

5% of 45   = 2.25

So 15% of 45 = 6.75

● Point out that, when working with money,
1% of £1 is 1p,
and so 23% of £7 is 7 × 23p = £1.61

INDIVIDUAL WORK

Students work through *Part 1* of the classwork sheet.

WORKING INTERACTIVELY

● Discuss how you can work out percentage change without a calculator (the scale factor idea using a calculator is in lesson 21).

e.g.   £45 increased by 20% is £45 + £9 = £54

$\left(£9 \text{ is } \frac{1}{5} \text{ of } £45\right)$

15% off £35 in a sale: 10% is £3.50

5% is £1.75

15% is £5.25

Sale price is £35 − £5.25 = £29.75

● VAT (Value Added Tax) is 17.5%. Why? Maybe because it is easy to work out without a calculator:

17.5% = 10% + 5% + 2.5%

Example: What is the VAT on a bill of £64?

10%   £ 6.40

5%   £ 3.20

2.5%   £ 1.60

17.5%   £11.20

So the total bill is £64 + £11.20 = £75.20

INDIVIDUAL WORK

Students work through the rest of the classwork sheet.

Review

Mark any classwork and review key strategies:

● Find percentages of quantities:

e.g. 17% of 40 = $\frac{17}{100} \times 40 = \frac{680}{100} = 6.8$

● Look for quick methods: e.g. 15% = 10% + 5%.
So, 15% off £35 = £35 − £3.50 − £1.75 = £29.75

● In particular, VAT at 17.5% is 10% + 5% + 2.5%.
So, VAT on a bill of £48 is
£4.80 + £2.40 + £1.20 = £8.40

ANSWERS TO THE CLASSWORK SHEET

Part 1

1 (a) 8 (b) 56 (c) 33 (d) 4.2 (e) 16 (f) 36

2 (a) 3 (b) 9 (c) 3

3 (a) £5.40 (b) £210 (c) £3.48 (d) £340
(e) £301 (f) £2.80 (g) £64.50 (h) £48 (i) £11

Part 2

1 Calculator: £14; Radio: £31.50; Television: £161

2 (a) 500 (b) 128 (c) 168 (d) 642 (e) 22.5 (f) 490

3 (a) 300 (b) 32 (c) 91 (d) 273 (e) 11.5 (f) 65

4 (a) Tyre: £7; Front door: £367.50; Car: £1837.50
(b) Tyre: £47; Front door: £2467.50; Car: £12 337.50

HOMEWORK

Page 66

HOMEWORK ANSWERS

Page 135

20 Finding percentages without a calculator

 Do not use a calculator

Part 1

1 Calculate these amounts.

(a) 4% of 200   (b) 7% of 800   (c) 11% of 300

(d) 3% of 140   (e) 5% of 320   (f) 8% of 450

2 Copy and complete these calculation, replacing each ? by a number.

(a) ?% of 400 = 12   (b) ?% of 800 = 72   (c) ?% of 230 = 6.9

3 Calculate these amounts.

(a) 18% of £30   (b) 35% of £600   (c) 87% of £4

(d) 40% of £850   (e) 7% of £4300   (f) 3.5% of £80

(g) 15% of £430   (h) 60% of £80   (i) 25% of £44

Part 2

1 The prices of all items in a sale are decreased by 30%. These are the prices before the sale.

Calculator	**£20**
Radio	**£45**
Television	**£230**

What are the sale prices?

2 Increase each of these amounts by the percentage shown.

(a) 400 by 25%   (b) 80 by 60%   (c) 120 by 40%

(d) 600 by 7%   (e) 15 by 50%   (f) 280 by 75%

3 Decrease each of these amounts by the percentage shown.

(a) 400 by 25%   (b) 80 by 60%   (c) 130 by 30%

(d) 300 by 9%   (e) 23 by 50%   (f) 260 by 75%

4 These are the prices of items without VAT.

Tyre	**£40**
Front door	**£2100**
Car	**£10 500**

(a) VAT is charged at 17.5%. Work out the VAT on each of these items.

(b) Find the total cost of each item, including VAT.

20 Finding percentages without a calculator

 **Do not use a calculator**

1 Calculate these amounts.

(a) 2% of 600   (b) 9% of 700

(c) 17% of 200   (d) 4% of 130

(e) 5% of 480   (f) 15% of 320

2 Copy and complete these calculation, replacing each ? by a number.

(a) ?% of 800 = 32   (b) ?% of 600 = 54

(c) ?% of 1000 = 350 (d) ?% of 50 = 2

(e) ?% of 140 = 4.2

3 Calculate these amounts.

(a) 16% of £600   (b) 65% of £900

(c) 93% of £6   (d) 70% of £1300

(e) 9% of £3500   (f) 15% of £690

(g) 75% of £56   (h) 3.5% of £8000

(i) 0.3% of £670

4 A shop has to increase its prices by 10%. What is the new price for

(a) a pencil costing 90p?

(b) a CD costing £13?

5 Another shop decreases its prices by 15% in a sale. What are the sale prices for

(a) a pair of trousers costing £29?

(b) a pair of trainers costing £65?

6 Increase each of these amounts by the percentage shown.

(a) 40 by 25%

(b) 1000 by 42%

(c) 27 by 50%

7 Decrease each of these amounts by the percentage shown.

(a) 250 by 60%

(b) 225 by 20%

(c) 460 by 75%

8 Find the price of each of these items. VAT is charged at 17.5%.

(a) Car tyre: £72 + VAT

(b) Office chair: £84 + VAT

(c) Computer: £350 + VAT

(d) Washing machine: £790 + VAT

(e) Car: £14 800 + VAT

21 Finding percentages with a calculator

LESSON OBJECTIVES

● Understand the multiplicative nature of percentages as operators
● Solve percentage problems involving increase and decrease
● Use calculators for percentage problems

WORKING INTERACTIVELY

● Remind students that $53\% = \frac{53}{100}$, and so on.
● What is 53% of £450? On a calculator work out
  $53 \div 100 \times £450 = £238.50$.
  The '÷ 100' is equivalent to '%'.
  (Do *not* use the % button.)
● Check students can work out:
  32% of £56   (= £17.92)
  47% of 550 litres   (= 258.5 litres)
  39% of 1250 metres   (= 487.5 metres)

INDIVIDUAL WORK

Students work through *Part 1* of the classwork sheet.

WORKING INTERACTIVELY

● Increase £45 by 20%. One way to do this is to find
  20% of £45 and add it on.
  But another way is to use a **multiplier**. Multiply £45
  by 1.20. Discuss why this works. (Answer is £54)
● Increase 3.5 kg by 6%. This time multiply by 1.06.
  Discuss why. (Answer is 3.71 kg)
● Decrease £30 by 10%. One way is to find 10% and
  subtract it. But the **multiplier** 0.90 gives the same
  result (£27).
  What multiplier is need to:
  increase a quantity by 60%   (1.6)
  increase a quantity by 3%   (1.03)
  decrease a quantity by 60%   (0.4)
  decrease a quantity by 3%?   (0.97)

INDIVIDUAL WORK

Students work through the rest of the classwork sheet.

HOMEWORK

Page
69

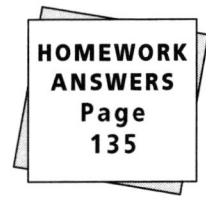

HOMEWORK
ANSWERS
Page
135

Review

Mark any classwork and review strategies:
● 32% of £56 = £(32 ÷ 100 × 56)
● To increase £72 by 18%, calculate £72 × 1.18
● To decrease £72 by 18%, calculate £72 × 0.82

ANSWERS TO THE CLASSWORK SHEET

Part 1
1   £263.20
2   5.88 kg
3   £3.72
4   £21.70
5   £3.24
6   448.2 m

Part 2
1

Percentage change	Multiplier
Increase by 20%	× 1.20
Increase by 30%	× **1.30**
Decrease by 40%	× 0.60
Decrease by 70%	× **0.30**
Increase by 40%	× **1.40**
Decrease by 10%	× **0.90**
Decrease by 35%	× **0.65**
Increase by 17.5%	× **1.175**
Decrease by 25%	× 0.75
Increase by 12.5%	× 1.125

2   (a) 392   (b) 336   (c) 252   (d) 308   (e) 810   (f) 630
3   308 ml
4   Yes, more than 15% free (15% extra is 253 g).
5   £9.75

21 Finding percentages with a calculator

You need a calculator

Part 1

Calculate these.

1 47% of £560

2 21% of 28 kg

3 3% of £124

4 17.5% of £124

5 72% of £4.50

6 54% of 830 metres

Part 2

1 Copy and complete this table.

Percentage change	Multiplier
Increase by 20%	× 1.20
Increase by 30%	
Decrease by 40%	× 0.60
Decrease by 70%	
	× 1.40
	× 0.90
Decrease by 35%	
Increase by 17.5%	
	× 0.75
	× 1.125

2 **(a)** Increase 350 by 12%.

(b) Decrease 525 by 36%.

(c) Decrease 840 by 70%.

(d) Decrease 560 by 45%.

(e) Increase 720 by 12.5%.

(f) Decrease 720 by 12.5%.

3 A drink can contains 275 ml. The size is increased by 12%. How much drink does it now contain?

4 A can of beans normally contains 220 g. In a special offer the can claims to offer 15% extra free. The new can contains 260 g. Is the claim justified?

5 In a sale CDs are sold at 35% off. What is the price of a CD normally costing £15?

21 Finding percentages with a calculator

You need a calculator

1 What is
  (a) 37% of £650?
  (b) 24% of 85 kilometres?
  (c) 17.5% of £599?
  (d) 2.7% of £1300?

2

ELECTRIC POWER SHOPS 30% OFF ALL GOODS	SUPERSAVER STORES $\frac{1}{3}$ OFF ALL GOODS

You want to buy a stereo cassette player which usually costs £170.
Find how much it would cost in each shop.

3 Copy and complete this table of percentage changes and multipliers.

Percentage change	Multiplier
Increase by 5%	× 1.05
	× 0.92
Decrease by 25%	
	× 1.2
	× 1.5
Decrease by 34%	
	× 0.90
	× 0.875
	× 2

4 Use a multiplier to work each of these out.
  (a) Increase £55 by 20%
  (b) Increase £72 by 12%
  (c) Decrease £66 by 30%
  (d) Decrease £85 by 18%
  (e) Increase £130 by 77%
  (f) Decrease £130 by 77%

5 A car hire firm works out its charges in three parts.
    A fixed fee of £28.45
    A rate of 12.5p per mile travelled
    Value Added Tax at 17.5% added on to the total cost

A man hires a car from this firm and travels 260 miles. How much will he have to pay?

22 Finding one quantity as a percentage of another

LESSON OBJECTIVES

- Find one quantity as a percentage of another
- Use percentages to compare proportions
- Use calculators for percentage problems

WORKING INTERACTIVELY

- What percentage of this class is female? Discuss how to find this – calculate the result to the nearest 1%.

- In another class 17 out of 31 students are female. What percentage are female?
  $17 \div 31 \times 100 = 54.8$. So the percentage is 55% to the nearest 1%.

- What percentage of the people in this room are wearing glasses?

INDIVIDUAL WORK

Students work through *Part 1* of the classwork sheet.

WORKING INTERACTIVELY

- A tin of beans costs 21p. In a special offer, it is reduced to 17p.

  What is the percentage reduction?

  The actual reduction is 4p.

  So, the percentage reduction is
  $\frac{4}{21} \times 100 = 19.047\,61$
  The reduction is 19%, to the nearest whole number.

- A woman bought a bike for £40, reconditioned it at a cost to her of £13.50 and resold it for £65. What percentage profit did she make on her total cost?

  The actual profit is £65 – £40 – £13.50 = £11.50

  Percentage profit = $11.50 \div 53.50 \times 100\%$
  $= 21.495\%$
  or 21% to the nearest per cent.

INDIVIDUAL WORK

Students work through the rest of the classwork sheet.

Review

Mark any classwork and review strategies:

- To find one number (x) as a percentage of another number (y) work out $\frac{x}{y} \times 100\%$

- If the two numbers are in different units put them into the same units first.

ANSWERS TO THE CLASSWORK SHEET

Part 1

1	63%
2	46%
3	65%
4	90%
5	70%
6	62%
7	69%
8	57%
9	57%

Part 2

1	30%
2	91%
3	4%
4	108%
5	60%
6	**(a)** 2759 **(b)** 1586 **(c)** 57%

HOMEWORK

Page
72

HOMEWORK
ANSWERS
Page
135

Finding one quantity as a percentage of another

You need a calculator

Part 1

Change these marks to percentages, to the nearest 1%.

1 38 out of 60

2 37 out of 80

3 97 out of 150

4 63 out of 70

5 84 out of 120

6 156 out of 250

7 76 out of 110

8 43 out of 76

9 54 out of 95

Part 2

1 A school has 869 students. 257 of the students walk to school. What percentage of students walk to school?

2 A theatre has seats for 2370 people. At a particular performance there were 2158 people. What percentage of the seats were filled?

3 A musician earns 57p for every CD sold. CDs sell for £14.00. What percentage of the price does the musician earn?

4 Anne bought an old table for £25, mended it and smartened it up and sold it for £79.90. The materials she used to improve the table cost her £13.50. What was the percentage profit on the total cost?

5 Sharon bought a car for £13 599 and three years later sold it for £5400. What was the percentage loss?

6 Here are five readings of Ben's electricity meter.

3rd April 1999	20 589
3rd July 1999	21 167
3rd October 1999	21 762
3rd January 2000	22 518
3rd April 2000	23 348

(a) How many units of electricity did Ben use between 3rd April 1999 and 3rd April 2000?

(b) How many units of electricity did Ben use between 3rd October 1999 and 3rd April 2000?

(c) What percentage of the electricity used during the year between 3rd April 1999 and 3rd April 2000 was used during the two winter quarters (3rd October 1999 to 3rd April 2000)?

22 Finding one quantity as a percentage of another

You need a calculator

1 A bag contains 75 chocolates, 36 of which are plain chocolates. The rest are milk chocolates.
What percentage of the chocolates are milk chocolates?

2 This table gives information about the members of a chess club.

	Men	Women
Wear glasses	17	11
Do not wear glasses	9	13

(a) What percentage of the members are women?

(b) What percentage of the men wear glasses?

3 Turn these homework marks into percentages.

(a) 23 out of 40

(b) 43 out of 60

(c) 87 out of 150

4 In the Run Fast club 8 out of 10 members have run a marathon.

In the Keep Going Somehow club 85% of members have run a marathon.

Which of the clubs is more impressive in this regard?

5 In a survey, 260 men and 213 women were asked whether they enjoyed gardening.

65 of the men and 58 of the women said they enjoyed gardening.

On the basis of this survey, is gardening more popular with men or with women?

6 Gaddesby United team won 14 out of its 18 football matches. Rearsby Rovers won 17 out of a total of 25 of its football matches. Which of the two teams won the higher percentage of matches?

7 A shop raised the price of a television costing £265 by £35 and a CD player costing £165 by £25. On which item was the percentage price rise higher?

8 A radio phone-in asks the question:

Do you think that men do as much cooking as women?

Out of a total of 26 384 calls, 14 478 were from men and the rest were from women.

Of the men, 6428 said yes and the rest said no. Of the women, 6132 said yes and the rest said no.

Did a higher percentage of the men than women think that men do as much cooking as women?

23 Repeated percentage change

LESSON OBJECTIVES

- Understand the multiplicative nature of percentages as operators
- Represent repeated percentage change using a multiplier raised to a power
- Solve percentage problems involving increase and decrease
- Use calculators for percentage problems

WORKING INTERACTIVELY

- If you put £400 in the bank and the bank pays you 7% interest p.a. (per year), how much will you have after three years? (This is called **compound interest**.) Here is one way of doing the calculation.

  After the first year:
  £400 + £28 = £428
  After the second year:
  £428 + 7% of £428 = £428 + £29.96 = £457.96
  After the third year:
  £457.96 + 7% of £457.96 = £457.96 + £32.06 = **£490.02**

  But, as was explained in lesson 21, to increase something by 7% it is quicker to multiply by 1.07. Use this method to check the answer to the calculation above.

  Point out that the whole calculation can be written as £400 × 1.07^3.
  Now consider after how many years the savings reach £600. (Keep multiplying by 1.07; it takes 6 years to reach £600.29)

- Decrease 160 by 50%. Now decrease it by 50% again. Is the answer a surprise? Do this again and again. Does the answer ever reach zero? (Answers: 80; 40; no)

- The value of a car decreases by 20% per year. When new it is worth £20 000. How much is it worth after 5 years? (£6553.60, or a sensible approximation!)

- If you increase by 20% and then decrease by the same percentage, do you get back to the same number? Students could suggest a number to test. You could then point out that you do not need a number to test: the multiplying factor is 1.20 × 0.80 = 0.96, giving a 4% decrease on the original number.

  A price increases by 10% and then decreases by 5%. What is the overall percentage change?
  1.10 × 0.95 = 1.045. So, a 4.5% increase.

INDIVIDUAL WORK

Students work through the classwork sheet.

Review

Mark any classwork and review key strategies:

- Use a multiplier for percentage increase or decrease. For example 1.06 for increase of 6% and 0.88 for a decrease of 12%.

- For repeated percentage increase or decrease, multiply the multipliers together.
  For an annual increase of 6% over three years, multiply by 1.06^3
  For an annual decrease of 12% over four years, multiply by 0.88^4
  For an increase of 5% followed by a decrease of 10%, multiply by 1.05 × 0.90 = 0.945. So this is equivalent to an overall decrease of 5.5% (1 − 0.945 = 0.055).

ANSWERS TO THE CLASSWORK SHEET

1 (a) £408.15 (b) £108.15 (c) 9 years (£599.70), 10 years (£647.68)

2 (a) £5520 (b) £4700

3 (a) £91 400 (to nearest £100) (b) 15 years

4 (a) 4 years (1.2^4 = 2.07) (b) 8 years (1.1^8 = 2.14)
  (c) 15 years (1.05^{15} = 2.08)

5 About 7% (1.10 × 0.92 × 1.06 = 1.0727)

6 No, 1% lower (1.10 × 0.90 = 0.99)

7 First bank. 1.014^{12} = 1.1816, which is 18.16% per year.

HOMEWORK

Page 75

HOMEWORK ANSWERS

Page 136

---

23 Repeated percentage change

You need a calculator

1. A special savings account pays 8% interest per annum. You invest £300 in the account.
   (a) How much is in your account after four years?
   (b) How much interest has your account earned in the four years?
   (c) How many years would you need to leave the money in the account for it to double?

2. A motor bike depreciates in value 15% each year. When new the motor bike cost £8500.
   (a) How much is it worth after three years?
   (b) A man sells the bike after five years. How much money has he lost on the bike altogether, to the nearest £100?

3. Mr and Mrs Jones buy a house for £75 000. It is predicted that house prices will rise by 2% each year. If the prediction is correct,
   (a) how much will the house be worth after 10 years?
   (b) after how many years will the house be worth £100 000?

4. How long will it take your savings to double if you invest at an interest rate of
   (a) 20% per annum?
   (b) 10% per annum?
   (c) 5% per annum?

5. A shop increases its prices by 10%, then reduces them by 8% and then increases them by 6%. What is the overall change in the prices?

6. A shop increases its prices by 10% and then reduces them by 10%. Are the prices back where they started?

7. A bank charges 18% per year to borrow money.
   Another bank charges 1.4% per month.
   You want to borrow some money for a year. Which is the better deal?

Lessons in Numeracy (Intermediate) © Longman (an imprint of Pearson Education) 2001

23 Repeated percentage change

You need a calculator

1 A settee is priced at £570. During the year its price increases by 5%, decreases by 20% and then increases by 10%.
  (a) What is the final price?
  (b) What is the overall percentage change?

2 A saleswoman earned £8500 for the year ending December 1996. Each year she was given a wage rise of 4%. How much did she earn for the year ending December 1999?

3 £500 is invested for 2 years at 6% per annum compound interest.
  (a) Work out the total interest earned over the two years.
  £250 is invested for 3 years at 7% compound interest.
  (b) By what single number must £250 be multiplied to obtain the total amount after 3 years?

4 A new car costs £14 000. Each year its value decreases by about 12%.
  (a) About how much will the car be worth after one year?
  (b) A woman buys one of these cars, keeps it for three years and then sells it. How much money would you expect her to have lost?

5 The sides of a rectangle measure 4 cm and 3 cm.
  Both lengths are increased by 10%.
  (a) Find the new area.
  (b) What is the percentage increase in the area?

6 In a sale, a teapot was reduced by 20% from its original price of £9.50. I bought it on the last day of the sale, when there was a further 30% reduction in the sale prices.
  (a) How much did I pay for the teapot?
  (b) What percentage reduction did I get altogether?

7 Prices in a stationery store are decreased by 8%, then increased by 5% and finally increased by 10%. What is the overall percentage change?

8 Prices in a DIY store are increased by 8%, then decreased by 10% and finally decreased by 5%. What is the overall percentage change?

24 Reverse percentages

LESSON OBJECTIVES

● Calculate an original amount when given the transformed amount after a percentage change

● Use the percentage multiplier to solve reverse percentage problems

● Use calculators for percentage problems

● Select and use suitable strategies to solve problems involving percentages

---

WORKING INTERACTIVELY

Example 1: A young man pays 35% of his wages to his parents for his keep. One week he pays them £41.30. What did he earn that week?

Method 1: Finding 35% is equivalent to × 0.35.
So reverse this (÷ 0.35).
£41.30 ÷ 0.35 = £118

Method 2: 35% of his wages is £41.30
So 1% of his wages is £41.30 ÷ 35.
So 100% of his wages is
£41.30 ÷ 35 × 100 = £118

Example 2: A bottle of shampoo is marked '20% extra free'. It contains 120 ml. How many ml are in the usual size bottle?
Most students know the answer is 100 ml.

Method 1: Increase by 20% is equivalent to × 1.20.
So you have to reverse this: ÷ 1.20.
120 ml ÷ 1.20 = 100 ml

Method 2: 120% of the usual bottle is 120 ml.
So 1% of the usual bottle is 1 ml.
So 100% of the usual bottle is 100 ml.

Note that Method 1 is the method suggested by the GCSE specifications, although for questions such as Example 1, Method 2 may be simpler to understand.

Example 3: The local bus company offers a 15% discount to students. A student pays £5.44 for a journey. What is the full fare for that journey?

Method 1: To get 15% discount you do × 0.85.
So full fare is £5.44 ÷ 0.85 = £6.40.

Method 2: 85% of full fare is £5.44.
So 1% of full fare is £5.44 ÷ 85.
So 100% of full fare is
£5.44 ÷ 85 × 100 = £6.40.

Example 4: SALE 30% OFF! Jeans £56 in sale.

What was the price of the jeans before the sale? (£56 ÷ 0.70 = £80)

Example 5: A drink can offers '13% extra free'. The volume of drink in the can is 500 ml. What was the volume of drink in the can before this free offer?
(500 ÷ 1.13 = 440 ml (sensible rounding))

Example 6: A restaurant bill, including VAT, comes to £39.71. What was the bill before VAT was added on?
(£39.71 ÷ 1.175 = £33.80)

INDIVIDUAL WORK

Students work through the classwork sheet.

Review

Mark any classwork and review key strategies:

● If £41.30 is 35% of wages then
wages = £41.30 ÷ 0.35 = £118

● If the 15% discounted price is £5.44 then full price is £5.44 ÷ 0.85 = £6.40

● If the price including VAT is £49 then the price without VAT is £49 ÷ 1.175 = £41.70

● So to reverse a percentage change you *divide* by the multiplier.

ANSWERS TO THE CLASSWORK SHEET

1 (a) 24   (b) 40   **2** £25

3 Table £200, Cupboard £120, Chair £60, Rug £80

4 (a) £170   (b) £25.50

5 (a) Thiamin 1.3 mg, Riboflavin 1.5 mg, Niacin 18.4 mg, Vitamin B6 2 mg, Iron 14.4 mg   (b) Thiamin, Riboflavin, Vitamin B6, Iron, Niacin

6 Depending whether you round VAT up or down:
Tapes 44p or 45p, Videos £1.63 or £1.64, CDs 74p or 75p, Computer games £2.53 or £2.54

HOMEWORK
Page
78

HOMEWORK
ANSWERS
Page
136

24 Reverse percentages

You need a calculator

1 (a) When a number is increased by 25% the answer is 30. What was the original number?

(b) When a number is decreased by 25% the answer is 30. What was the original number?

2 In a sale all prices have been reduced by 10%.

The sale price of a shirt is £22.50. What was the original price?

3 These prices include VAT, charged at 17.5%. What are the original prices?

Table	**£235**	**Cupboard**	**£141**
Chair	**£70.50**	**Rug**	**£94**

4 A musician's agent deducts 15% of earnings before giving the musician his money. The musician receives £144.50.

(a) What is the pay?

(b) How much does the agent get?

5 A breakfast cereal packet contains this information about the nutrients in 40 g of the cereal.

Nutrient	Amount in a 40 g portion of cereal	How much this is of recommended daily allowance
Thiamin	0.4 mg	30%
Riboflavin	0.6 mg	40%
Niacin	4.6 mg	25%
Vitamin B6	0.6 mg	30%
Iron	3.6 mg	25%

(a) How much of each nutrient is the recommended daily allowance?

(b) List the nutrients in order of recommended daily allowance, starting with the smallest.

6 In a sale, a shop wants to price various items at these prices, which include VAT at 17.5%.

Tapes	**£3**	**Videos**	**£11**
CDs	**£5**	**Computer games**	**£17**

How much VAT is there on each item?

24 Reverse percentages

You need a calculator

1 After the annual stock check, prices were increased by 8%. If these are the new prices, what were the old prices?

(a) £27   (b) £286.20

2 In a sale, all the goods were reduced by 30%.
If these are the new prices, what were they before the sale?

(a) £35   (b) £6.30

3 The special offer beer can was marked '25% extra'. It had 550 ml of beer in it. How much beer was in the original can?

4 A theatre offers 20% discount for students.

(a) The normal price for one show was £12.50.
What would a student pay?

(b) For another show a student paid £8.40.
What was the normal price for this show?

5 A breakfast cereal packet contains this information about the nutrients in 40 g of the cereal.

6 Between 1998 and 1999, the number of students in a school increased by exactly 28%.

The number of students in 1999 was 1984. What was the number in 1998?

7 A man bought a car which depreciated in value by 64%.

He sold it for £4500. How much did he pay for it?

8 After being given a pay rise of 8%, a woman earns £15 552 p.a.

What was her salary before the pay rise?

9 VAT is charged at 17.5%. The total charge for having a car serviced at a garage is £103.99, including VAT. How much of the cost is the VAT?

10 These prices all include VAT at 17.5%. What is the price of each item before VAT is added?

| *Shoes* | *£49* | *Shirt* | *£15* |
| *Coat* | *£85* | *Socks* | *£4.30* |

Nutrient	Amount of vitamin in 40 g of cereal	How much this is of recommended daily allowance
Vitamin C	39.6 mg	66%
Iron	3.6 mg	25%
Riboflavin	0.6 mg	40%
Thiamin	0.4 mg	30%

How much of each nutrient is the recommended daily allowance?

Lessons in Numeracy (Intermediate) © Longman (an imprint of Pearson Education) 2001

25 Rounding numbers

> ## LESSON OBJECTIVES
> - Round to the nearest integer
> - Round to the nearest 10, 100, 1000, etc.
> - Round to a given number of significant figures
> - Round to a given number of decimal places
> - Find upper and lower bounds of numbers given to a specified degree of accuracy

WORKING INTERACTIVELY

Discuss rounding to the nearest 10 100 and 1000 and to the nearest whole number.

- Round 82 km to the nearest 10 km.

- Round a height of 2657 ft to the nearest 100 feet.

- Round the attendance at a sporting event, 12 479, to the nearest 1000.

- Use a number line to demonstrate that, for example, 6.34 is nearer to 6.3 than to 6.4, but that 6.39 is nearer to 6.4.

- So   6.34 = 6.3   to **the nearest 0.1** or to **one decimal place.**

  and   6.39 = 6.4   to **the nearest 0.1** or to **one decimal place.**

- Note that 6.35 is half way between 6.3 and 6.4, but is usually rounded up to 6.4.

- Repeat the idea for 5.013 and 5.018 in relation to 5.01 and 5.02.

  So   5.013 = 5.01   to **the nearest 0.01** or to **two decimal places.**

  and 5.018 = 5.02   to **the nearest 0.01** or to **two decimal places.**

INDIVIDUAL WORK

Students work through *Part 1* of the classwork sheet.

WORKING INTERACTIVELY

- Discuss significant figures. Sometimes large numbers such as 7 248 729 need to be rounded. 7 248 729 is 'about 7 million'. This is correct to the nearest million. The approximation uses the 'most significant figure'.

- Significant figures are counted from the left.
  So, 7 248 729 is 7 000 000   to 1 significant figure
  7 248 729 is 7 200 000   to 2 significant figures
  7 248 729 is 7 250 000   to 3 significant figures
  0.005 369 is 0.005   to 1 significant figure
  0.005 369 is 0.0054   to 2 significant figures
  0.005 369 is 0.005 37   to 3 significant figures.

- What are these?
  0.0527 rounded to 2 decimal places   (0.05)
  0.0527 rounded to 2 significant figures   (0.053)
  5.8947 rounded to 3 decimal places   (5.895)
  5.8947 rounded to 3 significant figures   (5.89)
  435 879 rounded to 2 significant figures   (440 000)

INDIVIDUAL WORK

Students work through the rest of the classwork sheet.

WORKING INTERACTIVELY

- Ask students to draw a line in their exercise book and measure its length. Collect various results on board and discuss how accurately the lines have been measured and between what bounds the true lengths of the lines must lie.

- Example: 5 cm lies between 4.5 cm and 5.5 cm or, more precisely, if the length is L cm then $4.5 \leqslant L < 5.5$.
  4.5 is called the **lower bound** and 5.5 is called the **upper bound.**

- Example: If L is recorded as 7.2 cm then $7.15 \leqslant L < 7.25$.

- What are the lower and upper bounds of these?
  19 cm to the nearest cm   (18.5 cm and 19.5 cm)
  30 cm to the nearest cm   (29.5 cm and 30.5 cm)
  5.7 mm to the nearest 0.1 mm (5.65 mm and 5.75 mm)
  580 km to the nearest 10 km?   (575 km and 585 km)

- If a number is given as 14.3 correct to 1 decimal place, what could the number be?
  It could be anything between 14.25 and 14.35.

- What are the lower and upper bounds of these?
  87 rounded to the nearest whole number
  (86.5 and 87.5)
  34.62 rounded to 2 decimal places
  (34.615 and 34.625)
  5600 rounded to 2 significant figures
  (5550 and 5650)
  0.000 467 rounded to 3 significant figures
  (0.000 466 5 and 0.000 467 5)

Review

Mark any classwork and review significant strategies.

ANSWERS TO THE CLASSWORK SHEET

Part 1

1 (a) 50 m   (b) 350 m   (c) 100 m   (d) 1.38 km

2 (a) 1500 ft   (b) 900 ft   (c) 4600 ft   (d) 100 ft

3 (a) Monday 17 000, Tuesday 16 000, Wednesday 12 000, Thursday 1000, Friday 6000, Saturday 21 000   (b) Thursday

4 (a) 3.5   (b) 3.5   (c) 3.6   (d) 4.8

5 (a) 3.45   (b) 4.75   (c) 12.95   (d) 9.05

6 (a) 14.4   (b) 5.8   (c) 9.0   (d) 0.6

7 (a) 4.73   (b) 14.66   (c) 3.05   (d) 15.73

8 (a) 2.0   (b) 0.1   (c) 0.0   (d) 3.2

9 (a) 2.05   (b) 0.07   (c) 0.04   (d) 3.20

Part 2

1 (a) 29 0000   (b) 5700   (c) 56   (d) 0.080

2 (a) 28 600   (b) 5740   (c) 56.1   (d) 0.0800

3 (a) 28 000 people   (b) 46 cm   (c) 580 kg
   (d) 25 000 million acres   (e) 6000 yards   (f) 0.000 23 g

4 (a) 500 km   (b) 0.05 g   (c) 80 000 litres
   (d) 60 million people   (e) 8 miles

HOMEWORK

Page
82

HOMEWORK
ANSWERS
Page
136

Lessons in Numeracy (Intermediate) © Longman (an imprint of Pearson Education) 2001

25 Rounding numbers

Do not use a calculator

Part 1

1 Round each of these lengths to the nearest 10 metres.

    (a) 53 m   **(b)** 347 m   **(c)** 97 m   **(d)** 1.384 km

2 Round each of these heights to the nearest 100 feet.

    (a) 1493 feet   **(b)** 947 feet   **(c)** 4573 feet   **(d)** 53 ft

3 **(a)** These figures give the numbers of people who visited a theme park during a six-day period in summer. Round each of the numbers to the nearest 1000.

Monday:	*17 436*	*Tuesday:*	*15 729*
Wednesday:	*11 908*	*Thursday:*	*687*
Friday:	*6479*	*Saturday:*	*21 088*

    (b) On one of these days it rained heavily. Which day do you think that was?

4 Round each of these numbers to the nearest 0.1.

    (a) 3.46   **(b)** 3.52   **(c)** 3.58   **(d)** 4.84

5 What number is half way between these pairs of numbers?

    (a) 3.4, 3.5   **(b)** 4.7, 4.8   **(c)** 12.9, 13   **(d)** 9.0, 9.1

6 Round each of these numbers to 1 decimal place.

    (a) 4.36   **(b)** 5.78   **(c)** 9.04   **(d)** 0.62

7 Round each of these numbers to the nearest 0.01.

    (a) 4.732   **(b)** 14.657   **(c)** 3.048   **(d)** 15.725

8 Round each of these numbers to 1 decimal place.

    (a) 2.048 327   **(b)** 0.073 12   **(c)** 0.0406   **(d)** 3.197

9 Round each of these numbers to 2 decimal places.

    (a) 2.048 327   **(b)** 0.073 12   **(c)** 0.040 61   **(d)** 3.197

Part 2

1 Round each of these numbers to 2 significant figures.

    (a) 28 613   **(b)** 5741   **(c)** 56.1471   **(d)** 0.079 95

2 Round each of the numbers in question 1 to 3 significant figures.

3 Round each of these quantities to 2 significant figures.

    (a) 28 457 people   **(b)** 45.8 cm   **(c)** 583 kg

    (d) 24 567 million acres   **(e)** 6007 yards   **(f)** 0.000 234 67 g

4 Round each of these quantities to 1 significant figure.

    (a) 539 km   **(b)** 0.0483 g   **(c)** 76 000 litres   **(d)** 57 million people   **(e)** $7\frac{3}{4}$ miles

25 Rounding numbers

Do not use a calculator

1 These are the populations of three towns.
9300   265 300   1 477 000
Round each of the populations to the nearest thousand.

2 Round each of these numbers, correct to 2 decimal places.
  (a) 6.388   **(b)** 47.6449
  (c) 8.5555   **(d)** 78.103

3 Round each of these numbers to two decimal places.
  (a) 0.035   **(b)** 74.6549
  (c) 500.0039   **(d)** 0.004 268
  (e) 63.017   **(f)** 19.997

4 Round each of these numbers to three significant figures.
  (a) 687 908   **(b)** 0.004 985
  (c) 300.0037   **(d)** 338.5
  (e) 775 437.852 37   **(f)** 9.997

5 Round the number 648.791 25 to
  (a) 3 significant figures
  (b) 1 decimal place
  (c) the nearest 10
  (d) 3 decimal places
  (e) the nearest whole number

6 Round 8518.972 to
  (a) the nearest 10
  (b) the nearest hundred
  (c) one significant figure
  (d) one decimal place

7 Round each of these numbers to two decimal places.
  (a) 3.478   **(b)** 49.0848
  (c) 27.897   **(d)** 7.5555

8 Round each of these quantities to one significant figure.
  (a) 27 629 people   **(b)** 45.6 kg
  (c) 454 m   **(d)** 26 799 million gallons

9 Round each of these quantities to two significant figures.
  (a) 27 629 people   **(b)** 45.6 kg
  (c) 454 m   **(d)** 26 799 million gallons
  (e) $5\frac{2}{3}$ miles   **(f)** 0.000 478 4 m

10 Give the upper and lower bounds for these measurements.
  (a) 24 cm to the nearest cm
  (b) 40 cm to the nearest cm
  (c) 3.4 cm to the nearest 0.1 cm
  (d) 5.0 cm to the nearest 0.1 cm
  (e) 100 m to the nearest metre
  (f) 430 km to the nearest 10 km

26 Estimation and efficient use of a calculator

LESSON OBJECTIVES

- Round to a given number of significant figures
- Estimate answers to calculations involving decimals
- Use brackets and hierarchies of operations
- Use calculators efficiently for complex calculations
- Understand and interpret correctly the calculator display

WORKING INTERACTIVELY

- Remember the order for doing operations

  B   brackets

  I   indices (x^2, x^3, etc.)

  D   division

  M   multiplication

  A   addition   } working from

  S   subtractions } left to right

  $4 \times 8 - 3 \times 6 = 14$

  $5 \times 7 - (3 + 6) = 26$

  $7 + 3 \times 5^2 = 82$

  $\dfrac{13 - 12 \div 4}{4 + 3 \times 2} = 1$

- Check that students can estimate the answers to calculations like these:

5.88×312	(e.g. $6 \times 300 = 1800$)
$(9.85)^2 \times 15.6$	(e.g. $10^2 \times 15 = 1500$)
0.248×8.41	$\left(\text{e.g. } 0.25 \times 8 = \frac{1}{4} \times 8 = 2\right)$

- Check that students can use a calculator to work out these. Either get them to estimate first – or, after use of calculators (when they all get different answers) to see who is right!

  (Calculator answers are given to 3 significant figures, the same accuracy as numbers in questions.)

  $9.04 + (12.3 - 3.11^2)\,(= 9 + (12 - 9) = 12)\ \ (= 11.7)$

  $\dfrac{4.78 - 1.94^3}{5.63 + 0.42} \quad \left(= \left(\dfrac{5-8}{6}\right) = \dfrac{-3}{6} = -0.5\right)(= -0.417)$

  $\dfrac{6.21^2 + 1.79^2}{3.02^2 - 1.88^2} \quad \left(= \dfrac{6^2 + 2^2}{3^2 - 2^2} = \dfrac{40}{5} = 8\right)\ \ (= 7.48)$

INDIVIDUAL WORK

Students work through the classwork sheet.

Review

Mark any classwork and review key strategies including these:

- how to round numbers for estimating
- how to put calculations of the form $\dfrac{a+b}{c+d}$ into a calculator.

ANSWERS TO THE CLASSWORK SHEET

1 (a) $3 \times 2 = 6$ (b) $50 \times 0.2 = 10$ (c) $8000 \div 40 = 200$

(d) $600 \div 0.03 = 60\,000 \div 3 = 20\,000$

(e) $30 \times 0.06 = 1.8$

(f) $0.7 \times 2.5 \times 40 = 0.7 \times 100 = 70$

(g) $(10 \times 0.1) \div 2 = 1 \div 2 - 0.5$

(h) $(2 \times 0.5) \div 10 = 1 \div 10 = 0.1$

(i) $40 \div (5 \times 2) = 40 \div 10 = 4$

2 (a) 5.80 (b) 12.9 (c) 200 (d) 8900 (e) 2.12

(f) 74.4 (g) 0.469 (h) 0.0945 (i) 3.67

3 (a) $10 \div 5^2 = 10 \div 25 - 0.4$

(b) $(8 \times 3) \div (3 - 1) = 24 \div 2 = 12$

(c) $(8 \div 2^2) \div 1 = 8 \div 4 = 2$

(d) $15 - (3 - 1) = 15 - 2 = 13$

(e) $(20 + 2^3) \div (8 - 4) = 28 \div 4 = 7$

(f) $(20 - 8) \div 4 = 12 \div 4 = 3$

4 (a) 0.444 (b) 9.84 (c) 1.77 (d) 13.0 (e) 5.39 (f) 3.78

HOMEWORK	HOMEWORK ANSWERS
Page **85**	Page **136**

26 Estimation and efficient use of a calculator

Use a calculator only for questions 2 and 4

1 Estimate the answer for each of these.
   (a) 3.15×1.84
   (b) 52.1×0.248
   (c) $7958 \div 39.5$
   (d) $593.8 \div 0.0314$
   (e) 34.7×0.0612
   (f) $0.744 \times 2.52 \times 39.7$
   (g) $(9.69 \times 0.103) \div 2.13$
   (h) $(2.05 \times 0.475) \div 10.3$
   (i) $41.24 \div (4.88 \times 2.30)$

2 Use a calculator to work out the answer to each of the calculations in question 1. Give your answers correct to 3 significant figures.

3 Estimate the answer for each of these.
   (a) $\sqrt{103} \div (4.78)^2$
   (b) $\dfrac{7.84 \times 2.81}{3.28 - 1.04}$
   (c) $\dfrac{8.23 \div (2.17)^2}{0.985}$
   (d) $15.195 - (3.08 - 0.878)$
   (e) $\dfrac{16.72 + 2.12^3}{8.38 - 3.51}$
   (f) $\dfrac{23.76 - 8.19}{3.859 + 0.263}$

4 Use a calculator to work out the answer to each of the calculations in question 3. Give your answers correct to 3 significant figures.

Lessons in Numeracy (Intermediate) © Longman (an imprint of Pearson Education) 2001

26 Estimation and efficient use of a calculator

Do not use a calculator except for question 3

1 Estimate the answer to each of these calculations. Write down enough to show how you estimated your answer.

(a) 397×19

(b) $882 \div 28$

(c) 3.84×0.517

(d) $0.787 \div 0.195$

(e) $\sqrt{3.15^2 + 4.23^2}$

(f) $\dfrac{5.7}{12.2} + \dfrac{28.2}{57.6}$

2 Estimate the answer to each of these calculations. Write down enough to show how you estimated your answer.

(a) 489×2.08

(b) $376 \div 24.65$

(c) $\dfrac{18.2 \times 3.14}{5.99}$

(d) $\sqrt{2.06^3 + 1.93^3}$

(e) $\dfrac{5.9 + 4.23}{1.11 + 3.96}$

(f) $\dfrac{2.9^3}{13.7 - 4.9}$

3 Use a calculator to work out the answer to each of the calculations in questions 1 and 2. Give your answers correct to 3 significant figures.

4 Estimate, to one significant figure, the number of seconds in a century.

Lessons in Numeracy (Intermediate) © Longman (an imprint of Pearson Education) 2001

INTERMEDIATE ● HOMEWORK

26 Estimation and efficient use of a calculator

Do not use a calculator except for question 3

1 Estimate the answer to each of these calculations. Write down enough to show how you estimated your answer.

(a) 397×19

(b) $882 \div 28$

(c) 3.84×0.517

(d) $0.787 \div 0.195$

(e) $\sqrt{3.15^2 + 4.23^2}$

(f) $\dfrac{5.7}{12.2} + \dfrac{28.2}{57.6}$

2 Estimate the answer to each of these calculations. Write down enough to show how you estimated your answer.

(a) 489×2.08

(b) $376 \div 24.65$

(c) $\dfrac{18.2 \times 3.14}{5.99}$

(d) $\sqrt{2.06^3 + 1.93^3}$

(e) $\dfrac{5.9 + 4.23}{1.11 + 3.96}$

(f) $\dfrac{2.9^3}{13.7 - 4.9}$

3 Use a calculator to work out the answer to each of the calculations in questions 1 and 2. Give your answers correct to 3 significant figures.

4 Estimate, to one significant figure, the number of seconds in a century.

Lessons in Numeracy (Intermediate) © Longman (an imprint of Pearson Education) 2001

27 Trial and improvement

LESSON OBJECTIVES

- Use calculators effectively for complex calculations, including using the function key for powers
- Understand and interpret the calculator's display and know when, and when not, to round
- Use trial and improvement to solve number problems

WORKING INTERACTIVELY

The volume of a cube is 35 cm^3. Find the length of one edge, correct to 2 decimal places.

Consider the volumes of cubes with integer edge lengths, and thus show that the answer is between 3 cm and 4 cm. Then build up a table like this on the board, to find the volume by **trial and improvement**. Encourage students to use the power button on their calculators.

Guess for side of the cube (cm)	Volume of cube (cm^3)	Result
3.5	$3.5^3 = 42.875$	Too big
3.2	$3.2^3 = 32.768$	Too small
3.3	$3.3^3 = 35.937$	Too big
3.25	$3.25^3 = 34.328$	Too small
3.26	$3.26^3 = 34.646$	Too small
3.27	$3.27^3 = 34.966$	**Too small**
3.28	$3.28^3 = 35.288$	Too big
3.275	$3.275^3 = 35.126$	**Too big**

The last row is needed to be *sure* that the solution is 3.27 cm, rather than 3.28 cm.

A rectangle has a length which is 4 cm more than its width. Its area is 40 cm^2. Find the width of the rectangle, correct to 1 decimal place.

Students can suggest various integer values for the width and hence find that the width is between 4 cm ($4 \times 8 = 32$) and 5 cm ($5 \times 9 = 45$). A table like this will then help.

Guess for width (cm)	Length (cm)	Area (cm^2)	Result
4.5	8.5	$4.5 \times 8.5 = 38.25$	Too small
4.6	8.6	$4.6 \times 8.6 = 39.56$	**Too small**
4.7	8.7	$4.7 \times 8.7 = 40.89$	Too big
4.65	8.65	$4.65 \times 8.65 = 40.22$	**Too big**

So the width is between 4.6 cm and 4.65 cm and so is 4.6 cm, correct to 1 decimal place.

INDIVIDUAL WORK

Students work through the classwork sheet.

Review

Go through the problems on the classwork sheet.

ANSWERS TO THE CLASSWORK SHEET

1 3.7 and 5.7
2 65
3 4.73
4 4.7 cm
5 2.38 and 3.38

HOMEWORK

Page 88

HOMEWORK ANSWERS

Page 136

27 Trial and improvement

You need a calculator

1. One number is 2 more than another number. When you multiply the numbers the exact answer is 21.09. Use trial and improvement to find the two numbers.

2. Solve this number puzzle.

   I think of a number and then divide it by 2.5.
   Then I square the result.
   The answer is exactly 676.
   What number was I thinking of?

3. Solve the equation $y^4 = 500$, correct to 2 decimal places.

4. The length of a rectangle is 3 times the width. The area of the rectangle is 67 cm^2. Find the width of the rectangle, correct to 1 decimal place.

5. One number is 1 more than another number. Both of the numbers are cubed and the cubes are added. The result is exactly 52.095 744. What are the two numbers?

INTERMEDIATE ● CLASSWORK

27 Trial and improvement

You need a calculator

1. One number is 2 more than another number. When you multiply the numbers the exact answer is 21.09. Use trial and improvement to find the two numbers.

2. Solve this number puzzle.

   I think of a number and then divide it by 2.5.
   Then I square the result.
   The answer is exactly 676.
   What number was I thinking of?

3. Solve the equation $y^4 = 500$, correct to 2 decimal places.

4. The length of a rectangle is 3 times the width. The area of the rectangle is 67 cm^2. Find the width of the rectangle, correct to 1 decimal place.

5. One number is 1 more than another number. Both of the numbers are cubed and the cubes are added. The result is exactly 52.095 744.

Lessons in Numeracy (Intermediate) © Longman (an imprint of Pearson Education) 2001

27 Trial and improvement

You need a calculator

1. The volume of a cube is 40 cm³. Use trial and improvement to find the length of one edge, correct to 2 decimal places.

2. One number is 3 more than another number. When you multiply the two numbers the exact answer is 80.56. Use trial and improvement to find the two numbers.

3. Solve the equation $p^5 = 700$, correct to 1 decimal place.

4. Solve this number puzzle.

   I think of a number and then divide it by 3.6.
   I then cube the result.
   The answer is exactly 274.625.
   What number am I thinking of?

5. The length of a rectangle is 5 cm more than its width. The area of the rectangle is 80 cm². Find the width of the rectangle, correct to 1 decimal place.

6. One number is 2539 more than another number. The numbers are cube rooted and the sum of the cube roots is exactly 29. The smaller of the numbers is between 1950 and 1960. What are the two numbers?

Lessons in Numeracy (Intermediate) © Longman (an imprint of Pearson Education) 2001

INTERMEDIATE ● HOMEWORK

27 Trial and improvement

You need a calculator

1. The volume of a cube is 40 cm³. Use trial and improvement to find the length of one edge, correct to 2 decimal places.

2. One number is 3 more than another number. When you multiply the two numbers the exact answer is 80.56. Use trial and improvement to find the two numbers.

3. Solve the equation $p^5 = 700$, correct to 1 decimal place.

4. Solve this number puzzle.

   I think of a number and then divide it by 3.6.
   I then cube the result.
   The answer is exactly 274.625.
   What number am I thinking of?

5. The length of a rectangle is 5 cm more than its width. The area of the rectangle is 80 cm². Find the width of the rectangle, correct to 1 decimal place.

6. One number is 2539 more than another number. The numbers are cube rooted and the sum of the cube roots is exactly 29. The smaller of the numbers is between 1950 and 1960. What are the two numbers?

Lessons in Numeracy (Intermediate) © Longman (an imprint of Pearson Education) 2001

28 Time

WORKING INTERACTIVELY

Calendar

Make sure students know:

● the number of days in each month

● the number of days in a year and a leap year

● that a leap year is divisible by 4

● that when a date falls on a particular day it falls on the next day the following year, and explain why (because 365 days is 52 weeks and 1 day)

● what happens to the above in a leap year

● how to work out, for example, on what day Christmas Day will fall in 5 years' time (Tuesday in 2001)

● how to work out, for example, on what day their 18th birthday will fall.

Time

Make sure students know:

● that there are 60 seconds in a minute, 60 minutes in an hour, 24 hours in a day

● vocabulary of time (e.g. quarter past, half past, twenty to, …)

● how to convert between a.m./p.m. times and the 24-hour clock system

● that, for example, at 18:23 there are 37 minutes until 19:00

● that, for example, there are 3 hours 22 minutes between 10:45 and 14:07

Decimals of an hour

I used a calculator to work out a time in hours. I got 2.5 hours. What is this time in hours and minutes? (2 hours 30 minutes)

Repeat with more difficult examples: e.g. 3.1 hours (= 3 hours 6 minutes)

How could you use a calculator if you have a time like 2 hours 24 minutes? (Either use 2.4 hours or convert to 144 minutes.)

INDIVIDUAL WORK

Students work through the classwork sheet.

Review

Mark any classwork and review key strategies.

ANSWERS TO THE CLASSWORK SHEET

1

	1998	1999	2000	2001	2002	2003
Leap Year?	No	No	Yes	No	No	No
1st January	Thurs	Fri	Sat	Mon	Tues	Wed
5th November	Thurs	Fri	Sun	Mon	Tues	Wed

2 (a) Sunday (b) 2nd, 9th and 16th July

3 (a) 15 mins (b) 10 mins (c) 37 mins (d) 56 mins

4 (a) 45 mins (b) 3 hrs 30 mins (c) 4 hrs 35 mins (d) 2 hrs 30 mins

5 A: 16:25; B: 17:09; C: 16:00; D: 01:18

6 (a) 3 hrs 17 mins (b) 4 hrs 38 mins

7

Hours and minutes	Hours	Minutes
2 hours 15 minutes	2.25	135
3 hours 30 minutes	3.5	210
3 hours 42 minutes	3.7	222
1 hour 48 minutes	1.8	108
5 hours 20 minutes	5.33	320
2 hours 22 minutes	2.37	142
4 hours 35 minutes	4.58	275
52 minutes	0.87	52
2 hours 3 minutes	2.05	123
16 hours 40 minutes	16.67	1000

HOMEWORK

Page 91

HOMEWORK ANSWERS

Page 136

28 Time

 Do not use a calculator

1 Copy and complete this table

	1998	1999	2000	2001	2002	2003
Leap Year?			Yes			
1st January	Thurs			Mon		Wed
5th November						Wed

2 **(a)** In one non-leap year, January started on a Thursday.
On which day of the week did February begin?

(b) June 25th was a Thursday. Find the dates of the next three Thursdays.

3 For each of these, calculate how many minutes there are to the next o'clock time.

(a) 06:45 **(b)** 17:50 **(c)** 18:23 **(d)** 13:04

4 Calculate, in hours and minutes, the length of time between these.

(a) 12.15 p.m. and 1.00 p.m. **(b)** 10.45 a.m. and 2.15 p.m.

(c) 10:25 and 15:00 **(d)** 22:43 and 01:13

5 Look at this list of cinema programmes. Find the finishing time for each programme. Write your answer in 24-hour clock notation.

A: Starting time 13:55; length of programme 2 hours 30 minutes

B: Starting time 14:12; length of programme 2 hours 57 minutes

C: Starting time 11:52; length of programme 4 hours 8 minutes

D: Starting time 23:25; length of programme 1 hour 53 minutes

6 Write these as hours and minutes, correct to the nearest minute.

(a) 3.29 hours **(b)** 4.64 hours

7 Copy and complete this table.

Hours and minutes	Hours	Minutes
2 hours 15 minutes	2.25	135
		210
	3.7	
1 hour 48 minutes		
		320
	2.37	
4 hours 35 minutes		
	0.87	
		123
		1000

28 Time

 Do not use a calculator

1 Copy and complete this table

	1998	1999	2000	2001	2002	2003
25th December	Fri					
14th February					Thurs	

2 Calculate, in hours and minutes, the length of time between these.

(a) 8.30 a.m. and 9.15 a.m.

(b) 11.30 a.m. and 3.15 p.m.

(c) 06:15 and 11:35

(d) 16:23 and 20:13

3 Copy and complete this table.

Departure time	Travelling time (mins)	Arrival time
11:15	26	
12:46		13:03
14:25	37	
	55	13:50

4 A shopping trip in town is being planned.

Trains from Burford run into town at 8, 28 and 48 minutes past each hour.

The journey time is 46 minutes.

The shops open at 9.00 a.m. and shut at 5.30 p.m.

(a) What is the latest train from Burford that would allow 5 hours shopping before the shops shut?

(b) The return trains run every 20 minutes from 16:06.

What is the earliest train that the shoppers can catch after the shops close?

(c) If the shoppers managed to catch this train, at what time would they expect to arrive back in Burford?

5 Copy and complete this table.

Hours and minutes	Hours	Minutes
		150
2 hours 45 minutes		
	2.4	
		100
5 hours 20 minutes		
	3.85	

6 Write these as hours and minutes, correct to the nearest minute.

(a) 5.37 hours

(b) 2.84 hours

(c) 7.72 hours

29 Speed

LESSON OBJECTIVES

- Understand and use speed
- Develop a range of strategies for mental calculations involving speed
- Select appropriate strategies and techniques to solve problems involving speed
- Interpret solutions on a calculator display
- Give solutions to an appropriate degree of accuracy

WORKING INTERACTIVELY

- Start with simple questions that can be answered without a calculator and by using 'common sense'.

- A car travels 120 miles in 3 hours. What is its average speed? (120 ÷ 3 mph = 40 mph)

- A woman walks at four miles an hour for two hours. How far does she walk? (4 miles each hour, so 8 miles)

- A man cycles at 12 miles per hour. How long will a journey of 18 miles take? (12 miles takes 1 hour, another 6 take half an hour, so 1 hour 30 minutes)

- A car travels at 75 miles per hour down a motorway. How far will it travel in:

2 hours $(2 \times 75 \text{ miles} = 150 \text{ miles})$
20 minutes $\left(\frac{1}{3} \times 75 \text{ miles} = 25 \text{ miles}\right)$

1 hour 30 minutes $\left(75 \text{ miles} + \frac{1}{2} \times 75 \text{ miles} = 112\frac{1}{2} \text{ miles}\right)$

2 hours 40 minutes $\left(150 \text{ miles} + \frac{2}{3} \times 75 \text{ miles} = 200 \text{ miles}\right)$

- Use this diagram to discuss rules for speed for the harder questions given below.

- A man travels from Leicester to Nottingham. His journey is 28 miles. He starts at 8.03 a.m. and arrives at 8.57 a.m. What is his average speed? (28 ÷ 54 miles per minute = 0.5185 × 60 miles per hour = 31 mph (approximately))

- A woman travels home 123 miles after seeing her aunt. She estimates that she can average 48 mph on the journey. If the estimate is correct, how long will the journey take? (2.56 hours – about $2\frac{1}{2}$ hours to an appropriate degree of accuracy)

- A man knows from experience that he can average 17 mph when he goes out for a bike ride. It is now 11.15 a.m. and he needs to get home by 1 p.m. How far can he expect to ride? (Time = 1 hr 45 mins = 1.75 hours. Distance = 17 × 1.75 miles = 30 miles approximately.)

INDIVIDUAL WORK

Students work through the classwork sheet.

Review

Mark any classwork and review strategies:
- Use common sense when you can.
- Otherwise, use the triangle to help you remember.

Speed = Distance ÷ Time
Distance = Speed × Time
Time = Distance ÷ Speed

- Remember to think carefully about the units.

ANSWERS TO THE CLASSWORK SHEET

1 5 mins
2 $7\frac{1}{2}$ miles
3 15 mph
4 500 mph
5 **(a) (i)** 6 miles **(ii)** 4 miles **(iii)** 1 mile **(b) (i)** 45 minutes **(ii)** 40 minutes **(iii)** 1 hr 10 mins
6 9 weeks (125 cm ÷ 2 cm per day = 62.5 days)
7 11.02 a.m. (127 miles ÷ 70 mph = 1.81 hrs = 1 hr 49 mins)
8 **(a)** 85 mph (96 miles ÷ 1.13 hrs)
   (b) 61 mph (96 miles ÷ 1.57 hrs)
   (c) 4.33 p.m. (Speed is 73 mph; 96 miles ÷ 73 mph = 1.32 hrs = 1 hr 19 mins)

HOMEWORK
Page 94

HOMEWORK ANSWERS
Page 136

Lessons in Numeracy (Intermediate) © Longman (an imprint of Pearson Education) 2001

29 Speed

Do not use a calculator for questions 1 to 6

1 A woman cycled one mile at 12 mph. How long did she take?

2 A bus averages 10 mph on its journey into town. The journey takes 45 minutes. How long is the journey?

3 Roger Bannister was the first person to run a mile in fractionally under 4 minutes. What was his average speed?

4 An aeroplane travels 750 miles in 90 minutes. What is its average speed?

5 **(a)** John cycles at 12 mph. How far has he gone after
   (i) half an hour?
   (ii) 20 minutes?
   (iii) 5 minutes?
   (b) How long does it take him to travel
   (i) 9 miles?
   (ii) 8 miles?
   (iii) 14 miles?

6 A sunflower grows at an average speed of 2 cm per day. How many weeks will it take to grow $1\frac{1}{4}$ metres?

You may use a calculator for questions 7 and 8

7 A motorist has 127 miles to travel down the motorway. She will travel at 70 mph unless there is a hold-up. She joins the motorway at 9.13 a.m. At what time can she expect to leave the motorway?

8 **(a)** A train leaves Yortown for London at 11.05 a.m. and arrives at 12.13 p.m. The distance travelled is 96 miles. What is the average speed of the train?
   (b) A slow train leaves Yortown for London at 11.35 a.m. and arrives at 1.09 p.m. What is the average speed of this train?
   (c) The average speed for the 3.14 p.m. train from London to Yortown is exactly half way between the average speeds for the two trains in parts **(a)** and **(b)**. When does this train arrive at Yortown?

29 Speed

Do not use a calculator for questions 1 to 7

1 Someone walks one mile in 20 minutes. What is their speed?

2 A car averages 40 mph on a journey. The journey takes $1\frac{1}{4}$ hours. How many miles does the car travel?

3 Someone can jog at 6 mph. How far will they go in 10 minutes?

4 An aeroplane travels at an average speed of 400 mph. How long will it take to travel 1000 miles?

5 A cyclist can travel at 15 mph and has a 25 mile journey. How long is the journey likely to take?

6 A car travels at an average speed of 30 mph.
  (a) How far would it travel in
    (i) $2\frac{1}{2}$ hours?
    (ii) 20 mins?
    (iii) 5 mins?
  (b) How long would it take to travel
    (i) 150 miles?
    (ii) 45 miles?
    (iii) 1 mile?

7 A bus takes 10 minutes for a journey of 4 miles.
  (a) Calculate the average speed of the bus.
  (b) How far might the bus travel in 1 hour 20 minutes?

You may use a calculator for questions 8 to 10

8 Calculate the average speed in miles per hour (mph) of each of these car journeys.
  (a) A journey of 224 miles taking 3 hour 30 minutes
  (b) A journey of 126 miles taking 2 hour 15 minutes

9 A jet aeroplane travelling a distance of 480 km is in flight for 50 minutes.
  (a) Calculate the average speed of the jet.
  (b) Calculate the distance the jet would travel at this speed in 1 hour 20 minutes.

10 Most people can walk comfortably at a speed of 2 m/s, and swim at a speed of 1 m/s.
  (a) How long would it take to cover 1 km walking, and 1 km swimming?
  (b) How far would I travel, if I kept walking for 30 minutes?

  How far would I swim if I kept swimming for 30 minutes?

30 Ratio

LESSON OBJECTIVES

- Use ratio notation including reduction to its simplest form
- Divide a quantity in a given ratio
- Select appropriate strategies to solve problems involving ratio

---

WORKING INTERACTIVELY

- Introducing the idea of scaling up or scaling down, but keeping quantities in the same ratio.

- Here are the ingredients for a recipe for 20 biscuits.
  50 g cooking fat   2 rounded teaspoons mixed spice
  120 g caster sugar   30 g currants
  1 egg   pinch salt
  240 g plain flour
  Rewrite the recipe so that it is suitable for 40 biscuits, for 30 biscuits, for 150 biscuits.
  A ratio can be simplified in the same way as a fraction. What is the ratio of sugar to flour in this recipe, in its simplest form? (1 : 2)
  What is the ratio of flour to sugar? (2 : 1)
  What is the ratio of fat to sugar? (5 : 12)
  Of fat to currants? (5 : 3)
  Of flour to currants? (8 : 1)
  How much sugar for 320 g flour? (160 g)
  How many currants? (40 g)

- Point out that the quantities must be in the same units before a ratio is calculated. So, ratio of 1 kg to 300 g is 1000 : 300 = 10 : 3.

INDIVIDUAL WORK

Students work through *Part 1* of the classwork sheet.

WORKING INTERACTIVELY

- Discuss how to divide a quantity in a given ratio by considering this example:
  Share £60 between three people in the ratio 3 : 4 : 5.
  The first person receives 3 shares, the second 4 shares and the third 5 shares.
  So altogether there are 3 + 4 + 5 = 12 shares.
  Each share is £60 ÷ 12 = £5.
  The first person gets 3 × £5 = £15, the second gets 4 × £5 = £20 and the third gets 5 × £5 = £25.

INDIVIDUAL WORK

Students work through *Part 2* of the classwork sheet.

Review

Mark any classwork and review key strategies for simplifying ratios and for dividing a quantity in a given ratio.

You might in particular check that students understand how to tackle question 5 of *Part 1*. They can solve this by trial and improvement, but some may

understand the algebraic solution, solving $\dfrac{20 + x}{48 + x} = \dfrac{2}{3}$

ANSWERS TO THE CLASSWORK SHEET

Part 1
1   (a) 4 : 3   (b) 3 : 4   (c) 2 : 1
2   27 males
3   (a) 1 : 4   (b) 3 : 8   (c) 3 : 5   (d) 3 : 8
4   140 (36 men and 36 women join)

Part 2
1   (a) £300, £700   (b) £280, £720   (c) £250, £350, £400
2   £13, £39
3   18, 36
4   6.25 litres
5   375 cm² (15 cm by 25 cm rectangle)

HOMEWORK

Page 97

HOMEWORK ANSWERS

Page 136

30 Ratio

 Do not use a calculator

Part 1

1 In a bag there are 16 red cubes and 12 blue cubes.

    (a) Write down the ratio of red cubes to blue cubes in its simplest form.

    (b) What is the ratio of blue cubes to red cubes?

    (c) 8 red cubes are added to the bag. What is the ratio of red cubes to blue cubes now?

2 In a chess club there are 18 males and 12 females. In a bridge club the ratio of males to females is exactly the same as in the chess club. There are 18 females in the bridge club. How many males are there?

3 What is the ratio of

    (a) 25p to £1? **(b)** 150 cm to 4 m? **(c)** 600 g to 1 kg? **(d)** 45 minutes to 2 hours?

4 At the end of 1999 a sports club had this membership: 20 men, 48 women.
In 2000 the membership of the club grew rapidly. It happened that equal numbers of men and women joined and nobody left. At the end of 2000 the ratio of men to women in the club was 2 : 3.
What was the total membership of the club at the end of 2000?

Part 2

1 Divide £1000 in the ratio

    (a) 3 : 7   **(b)** 7 : 18   **(c)** 5 : 7 : 8

2 Divide £52 between two brothers, so that one gets three times as much as the other.

3 One number is twice as big as another. The sum of the numbers is 54. What is each number?

4 Green paint is made by mixing 5 parts of yellow paint with three parts of blue paint. How much yellow paint is needed to make 10 litres of green paint?

5 A rectangle has sides in the ratio 3 : 5. The perimeter of the rectangle is 80 cm. What is the area of the rectangle?

    Lessons in Numeracy (Intermediate) © Longman (an imprint of Pearson Education) 2001

 30 Ratio

 Do not use a calculator for questions 1 to 6

1 In a college the ratio of left-handed students to right-handed students is 2 : 13. There are 400 left-handed students in the college. How many right-handed students are there?

2 **(a)** What fraction of this grid is shaded?

(b) What is the ratio of shaded squares to unshaded squares?

(c) How many more squares need to be shaded so that the ratio of shaded squares to unshaded squares is 5 : 7?

3 What is the ratio of
(a) 40p to £1.20?
(b) 80 cm to 4 m?
(c) 750 g to 1 kg?
(d) 20 minutes to 1 hour?
(e) 40 minutes to 2 hours?
(f) 16 hours to 1 day?

4 Divide £360 in the ratio 3 : 4 : 5.

5 The ratio of men to women to children at a concert is 2 : 3 : 1. There are 420 people at the concert. How many are men?

6 A photograph is enlarged in the ratio 2 : 5.
(a) The original photograph is 8 cm wide.
How wide is the enlargement?
(b) The enlargement is 30 cm long. How long is the original photograph?

You may use a calculator for questions 7 and 8

7 These are the ingredients for a recipe for a marshmallow cake to serve 12 people:

300 g	**marshmallows**
240 g	**biscuit crumbs**
80 g	**butter**
120 g	**cocoa powder**
100 g	**castor sugar**

(a) Calculate the amount of biscuit crumbs required to make a cake for 8 people.
(b) Calculate the amount of marshmallows needed to make a cake for 30 people.
(c) Write the ratio of weights of marshmallows to biscuit crumbs in its simplest terms.

8 **(a)** The lengths of the sides of a triangle are in the ratio 4 : 5 : 7. The perimeter of the triangle is 56 cm. What is the length of the longest side?
(b) A second triangle is drawn. It is the same shape but reduced in size. The length of the longest side is now 10.5 cm.
What is the perimeter of the second triangle?

31 Direct proportion

> ## LESSON OBJECTIVES
>
> ● Understand and use direct proportion
> ● Calculate an unknown quantity for quantities that vary in direct proportion
> ● Select appropriate strategies to solve problems involving proportion
> ● Use calculators effectively and efficiently

WORKING INTERACTIVELY

● Discuss simple examples of direct proportion
e.g.   2 bars of chocolate cost 60p.
What does 1 cost? What do 4 cost?

Key idea   If you treble the number of bars of chocolate you treble the cost.

If you halve the number of bars of chocolate you halve the cost and so on.

Discuss further examples. In these examples the simplest strategy is to find the cost (or whatever) for *one item* first.

e.g.   6 tickets cost £15. What do 5 tickets cost?
(£12.50)
5 books cost £26.50. What do 8 books cost?
(£42.40)
It takes 10 minutes to write 3 Christmas cards. How long does it take to write 52 cards?
(173 minutes, to the nearest minute)

● Ask students to draw this graph, which shows how much different numbers of 30p chocolate bars cost.

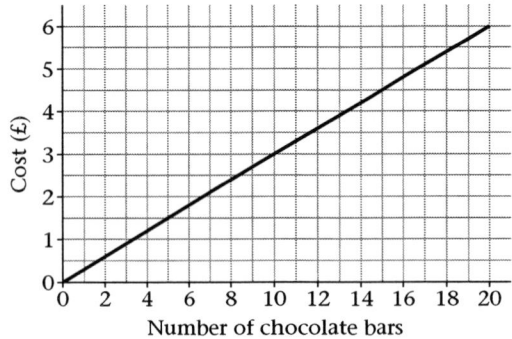

Number of chocolate bars

● Note that if two quantities are directly proportional the graph is a straight line through the origin.

● Discuss the fact that if you do not start with (0, 0) then the quantities are *not* directly proportional. For example, an electricity bill always consists of a fixed charge, in addition to a charge per unit. Explain that the consequence of this is the electricity bill is not directly proportional to the number of units used. *If you double the number of units you do not double the charge.*

● Now discuss this example:
A car salesman earns £240 a week basic salary, plus an extra £80 a week for every car he sells.
(a)   One week he earns £560. How many cars did he sell? (4 cars)
(b)   Another week he earns £240. How many cars did he sell? (no cars)
(c)   How many cars would he have to sell to earn £880? (8 cars)
Note that the answer to (c) is not twice the answer to (a); the quantities are not in direct proportion.

● Another application of direct proportion is 'best buys'. For example, a 200 ml bottle of shampoo costs £2.35, a 350 ml bottle of the same shampoo costs £3.99. Which is the best value?
(200 ml bottle costs 1.18 per ml; 350 ml bottle costs 1.14 p per litre. Or you can work out how much you get for 1p: 0.85 ml and 0.88 ml.)

Why might you not want to buy the better value bottle?

INDIVIDUAL WORK

Students work through the classwork sheet.

Lessons in Numeracy (Intermediate) © Longman (an imprint of Pearson Education) 2001

Review

Mark any classwork and review key strategies. Two
strategies are useful:

- If it is easy to see what one quantity has been
  multiplied by, do the same to the other quantity.
  For example,
  6 tickets cost £15. What do 9 tickets cost?
  9 is 1.5 × 6. So cost is 1.5 × £15 = £22.50

- Use the given information to find the cost (or
  whatever) for one item. For example,
  5 tickets cost £15. What do 7 cost?
  1 ticket costs £15 ÷ 5 = £3
  So 7 tickets cost 7 × £3 = £21.

- Remember that if quantities are in direct
  proportion, their graph is a straight line passing
  through the origin.

ANSWERS TO THE CLASSWORK SHEET

1 (a) Yes   (b) 10.8 francs   (c) 756 francs   (d) £85

2 £21.45

3 13.5 miles

4 (a) 120 mins   (b) 200 mins

5 250 g (250 g costs 1.44p per g; 200 g costs 1.49p per g. Or, in
250 g you get 0.69 g for 1p; in 200 g you get 0.67 g for 1p)

6 (a) 0.27p per g compared with 0.6p per g. Or, you get 3.7 g
for 1p compared with 1.7 g for 1p   (b) For example, the
large size could go stale before it is all eaten.

7 Box of 144 (In box of 60 each pencil costs 7.9p; in box of
144 each pencil costs 6.9p.)

8 (a)

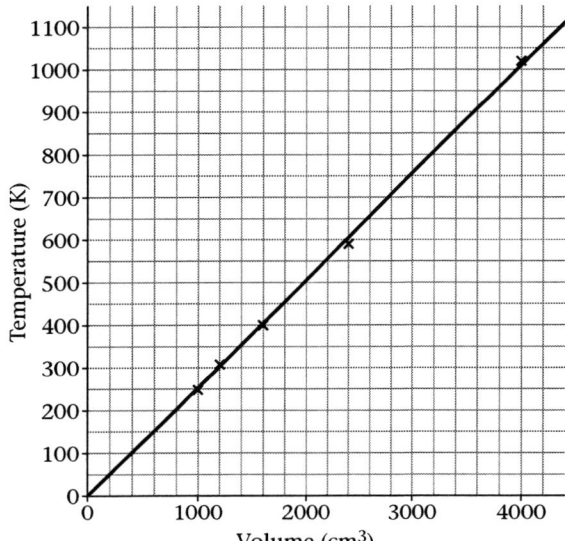

(b) Yes; straight-line graph through the origin

HOMEWORK

Page
102

HOMEWORK
ANSWERS
Page
137

31 Direct proportion

Do as many of these questions as you can without a calculator

1. This table shows the number of French francs you can buy for a pound at a particular travel agent.

Pounds (£)	2	4	5	10	20
Francs	21.6	43.2	54	108	216

   (a) Is the number of pounds directly proportional to the number of francs?

   (b) How many francs do you get for £1?

   (c) How many francs do you get for £70?

   (d) What is 918 francs worth in pounds?

2. Six receipt books cost £11.70. How much do 11 receipt books cost?

3. John cycles 9 miles in half an hour. If he travels at the same speed, how far will he cycle in 45 minutes?

4. It costs £15 a month plus 30p a minute to use a mobile phone. The bill for the month is £51.

   (a) For how many minutes was the phone used?

   (b) The bill for the whole year was £900. What was the average monthly use of the phone?

5. A 250 g jar of coffee costs £3.60, and a 200 g jar costs £2.98. Which is the best buy?

6. A 500 g box of breakfast cereal costs £1.35. A 150 g box of the same cereal costs 90p.

   (a) Explain why the larger size gives better value for money.

   (b) Why might some people still prefer to buy the smaller size?

7. A box of 60 pencils is sold for £4.75.
   A box of 144 similar pencils costs £9.99.
   Which box gives the best value for money?

8 A scientist carried out an experiment to determine the relationship between the volume (*V*) in cm³ and absolute temperature (*T*) in kelvins of a gas.

Here are some results.

Volume (*V*)	1000	1200	1600	2400	4000
Temperature (*T*)	248	308	400	590	1020

(a) Draw a graph to represent these results, using axes like these.

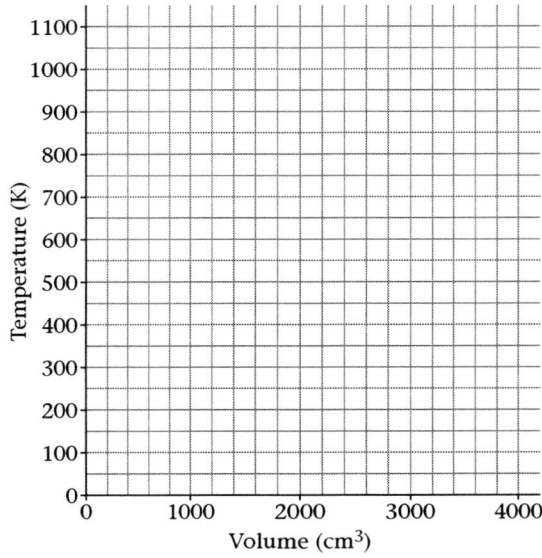

(b) Allowing for experimental error, do you think that *V* is directly proportional to *T*?

Give reasons for your answer.

31 Direct proportion

 **Do not use a calculator for questions 1 to 9**

1 You pay £28 for eight videos.
  (a) How much does one video cost?
  (b) How much do five videos cost?
  (c) How much do three videos cost?

2 The price of 4 litres of milk is £2.60.
  (a) What does 1 litre of milk cost?
  (b) What would 3 litres of milk cost?
  (c) What would 5 litres of milk cost?

3 Ten calculators cost £64.
  (a) What does one calculator cost?
  (b) What do three calculators cost?
  (c) What do 12 calculators cost?

4 The cost of 15 litres of petrol is £10.50. What is the cost of 10 litres of petrol?

5 Three CDs cost £34.50. What do four CDs cost?

6 Eight drinks cost £3.36. How much do three drinks cost?

7 It takes 20 minutes to travel 8 miles. How long would it take to travel 6 miles at the same speed?

8 A car saleswoman earns £200 a week basic salary, plus an extra £100 for every car she sells.
  (a) In week 1, she earns £600. How many cars did she sell?
  (b) In week 2, she earns £200. How many cars did she sell?
  (c) How many cars would she have to sell in one week to earn £1000?

9 A recipe for cooking beef says 'cook for 20 minutes per pound plus 30 minutes'. A man cooks a piece of beef for 1 hour 40 minutes. How much does the beef weigh?

You may use a calculator for questions 10 to 13

10 Hiring a car costs £32 a day plus 6p per mile.
  (a) In March, Anne hired the car for a day and paid £55.16. How many miles did she travel?
  (b) During the year, Anne hired the car on eight days. The total cost of the car hire for the year was £406.24. What was the average mileage per day?

11 A pack of 4 toilet rolls costs £1.65 and a pack of 9 of the same toilet rolls costs £3.35. Which size gives better value for money?

12 A supermarket has two makes of split red lentils. The first comes in 500 g bags which cost 75p. The second comes in 850 g bags which cost £1.35. Which size of bag is better value for money?

13 Two rival double glazing firms announce special offers on the same windows.
One company offers seven windows for £1995.
The other offers five windows for £1425. Which company is providing the best value for money?

32 Indices

WORKING INTERACTIVELY

Remind students of index notation that they have already met in lesson 10:

$$3^2 = 3 \times 3 \qquad 5^3 = 5 \times 5 \times 5 \qquad \text{etc.}$$

Discuss the meaning that can be attached to the zero power and negative powers by extending the pattern in this table. Encourage the use of fractions.

2^{-4}	2^{-3}	2^{-2}	2^{-1}	2^0	2^1	2^2	2^3	2^4
$\frac{1}{16}$	$\frac{1}{8}$	$\frac{1}{4}$	$\frac{1}{2}$	1	2	4	8	16

INDIVIDUAL WORK

Students work through *Part 1* of the classwork sheet.

WORKING INTERACTIVELY

Discuss results and, for the last table, say we shall meet these again when we do standard form in lessons 34 and 35.

● Stress that $x^0 = 1$ for *all x*, so for example:
$$538^0 = 1 \quad 8y^0 = 8, \quad (x^2 + y^2)^0 = 1$$

● Introduce the definition of **reciprocal** by considering, for example:

$$2^3 = 8 \text{ and } 2^{-3} = \frac{1}{8} \text{ and } 8 \times \frac{1}{8} = 1$$

$$3^4 = 81 \text{ and } 3^{-4} = \frac{1}{81} \text{ and } 81 \times \frac{1}{81} = 1$$

$$5^{-1} = \frac{1}{5} \text{ and } 5^1 = 5 \text{ and } \frac{1}{5} \times 5 = 1$$

So the reciprocal of any number N is $\frac{1}{N}$ or N^{-1}

(and the reciprocal of $\frac{1}{N}$ is N).

● Discuss how to find the reciprocal of these numbers:
$$\frac{1}{2} \qquad \frac{3}{4} \qquad 0.4 \qquad 3\frac{1}{2} \qquad \left(2 \quad \frac{4}{3} \quad 2.5 \quad \frac{2}{7}\right)$$
and confirm that a number multiplied by its reciprocal is always 1.

● Establish that:

the reciprocal of $\frac{a}{b}$ is $\frac{b}{a}$. So $\left(\frac{a}{b}\right)^{-1} = \frac{b}{a}$

the reciprocal of 1 is 1
the reciprocal of 0 does not exist.

INDIVIDUAL WORK

Students work through the rest of the classwork sheet.

Review

Mark any classwork and review strategies:

● $12^0 = 1 \qquad 5x^0 = 5 \qquad (ab)^0 = 1$
● $5^{-1} = \frac{1}{5} \qquad 3^{-4} = \frac{1}{3^4} = \frac{1}{81}$

● The reciprocal of 6 is $\frac{1}{6}$, of $\frac{1}{5}$ is 5, of $\frac{3}{7}$ is $\frac{7}{3}$.

● A number and its reciprocal multiply together to give 1.

● The reciprocal of 4^3 is 4^{-3} and of 9^{-4} is 9^4.

ANSWERS TO THE CLASSWORK SHEET

Part 1

1

3^{-4}	3^{-3}	3^{-2}	3^{-1}	3^0	3^1	3^2	3^3	3^4
$\frac{1}{81}$	$\frac{1}{27}$	$\frac{1}{9}$	$\frac{1}{3}$	1	3	9	27	81

2

5^{-4}	5^{-3}	5^{-2}	5^{-1}	5^0	5^1	5^2	5^3	5^4
$\frac{1}{625}$	$\frac{1}{125}$	$\frac{1}{25}$	$\frac{1}{5}$	1	5	25	125	625

3

10^{-4}	10^{-3}	10^{-2}	10^{-1}	10^0	10^1	10^2	10^3	10^4
$\frac{1}{10\,000}$	$\frac{1}{1000}$	$\frac{1}{100}$	$\frac{1}{10}$	1	10	100	1000	10 000

Part 2

1 (a) $\frac{1}{8}$ (b) $\frac{1}{4}$ (c) 20 (d) 3 (e) $\frac{8}{3}$ (f) $\frac{2}{5}$ (g) $\frac{4}{15}$

2 (a) 10 (b) 1.25 (c) $1.\dot{3}$

3 (a) $3^{-2} = \frac{1}{9}$ (b) $10^{-3} = \frac{1}{1000}$ (c) $4^{-3} = \frac{1}{64}$

(d) $2^3 = 8$ (e) $7^1 = 7$

HOMEWORK

Page
105

HOMEWORK
ANSWERS
Page
137

32 Indices

 **Do not use a calculator**

Part 1

Copy and complete these tables for powers of 3, 5 and 10.

1

3^{-4}	3^{-3}	3^{-2}	3^{-1}	3^{0}	3^{1}	3^{2}	3^{3}	3^{4}

2

5^{-4}	5^{-3}	5^{-2}	5^{-1}	5^{0}	5^{1}	5^{2}	5^{3}	5^{4}

3

10^{-4}	10^{-3}	10^{-2}	10^{-1}	10^{0}	10^{1}	10^{2}	10^{3}	10^{4}

Part 2

1 Find the reciprocal of each of these numbers. Give each answer as a whole number or as a fraction.

    (a) 8   **(b)** 4   **(c)** $\frac{1}{20}$ **(d)** $\frac{1}{3}$ **(e)** $\frac{3}{8}$ **(f)** $2\frac{1}{2}$ **(g)** $3\frac{3}{4}$

2 Find the reciprocal of each of these numbers. Give each as a whole number or a decimal.

    (a) 0.1   **(b)** 0.8   **(c)** 0.75

3 Find the reciprocal of each of these numbers. First, give each answer as a power, and then evaluate the power as a whole number or a fraction or a decimal.

    (a) 3^{2} **(b)** 10^{3} **(c)** 4^{3} **(d)** 2^{-3} **(e)** 7^{-1}

32 Indices

INTERMEDIATE ● HOMEWORK

32 Indices

Do not use a calculator

1 Write down the value of each of these.

(a) 6^0 (b) 1^0 (c) 25^0 (d) 4×5^0 (e) 15×8^0

(f) a^0 (g) $2x^0$ (h) $(p+q)^0$ (i) $p^0 + q^0$

2 Write down the value of each of these.

(a) 3^{-1} (b) 6^{-1} (c) 4^{-2} (d) 2^{-4}

(e) 5^{-2} (f) 2^{-5} (g) 7^{-2} (h) 9^{-1}

(i) 6^{-3} (j) 1^{-10} (k) $\left(\frac{1}{3}\right)^{-1}$ (l) $\left(\frac{2}{5}\right)^{-1}$

(m) $\left(\frac{1}{2}\right)^{-3}$ (n) $\left(\frac{2}{3}\right)^{-2}$ (o) $(1.3)^{-1}$

3 Find the reciprocal of each of these.

(a) 8 (b) 6 (c) 53 (d) 1

4 Find the reciprocal of each of these. Give your answers as mixed numbers.

(a) $\frac{2}{15}$ (b) $\frac{3}{5}$ (c) $\frac{5}{6}$ (d) $\frac{5}{12}$

5 Find the reciprocal of each of these. Give your answers as fractions.

(a) $2\frac{3}{4}$ (b) $7\frac{1}{3}$ (c) $2\frac{1}{3}$ (d) $3\frac{1}{7}$

6 Find the reciprocal of each of these. Give your answers as decimals.

(a) 0.4 (b) 0.25 (c) 1.25 (d) 1.6

33 Using indices

LESSON OBJECTIVES

● Use index notation and index laws for multiplication and division of integer powers
● Use index laws to simplify and calculate the value of numerical expressions

WORKING INTERACTIVELY

Use these and similar examples, with positive indices initially, to establish the rules for combining indices:

● $2^2 \times 2^3 = (2 \times 2) \times (2 \times 2 \times 2) = 2^5$

● $3 \times 3^5 = 3 \times (3 \times 3 \times 3 \times 3 \times 3) = 3^6$

● $4^5 \div 4^2 = \dfrac{4 \times 4 \times 4 \times 4 \times 4}{4 \times 4} = 4 \times 4 \times 4 = 4^3$

● $5^3 \div 5 = \dfrac{5 \times 5 \times 5}{5} = 5 \times 5 = 5^2$

● $(3^2)^3 = 3^2 \times 3^2 \times 3^2 = 3^6$

● $(5^3)^3 = 5^3 \times 5^3 \times 5^3 = 5^9$

These are laws of indices students need to know:

● When multiplying, add the indices:
$a^m \times a^n = a^{m+n}$

● When dividing, subtract the indices:
$a^m \div a^n = a^{m-n}$

● For powers of powers multiply the indices:
$(a^m)^n = a^{mn}$

● $a^0 = 1$ (from lesson 32)

● $a^{-1} = \dfrac{1}{a}$ (the reciprocal of a) and $a^{-m} = \dfrac{1}{a^m}$

(from lesson 32)

INDIVIDUAL WORK

Students work through *Part 1* of the classwork sheet.

WORKING INTERACTIVELY

Establish that the rules work if some or all of the indices are negative.

● $10^{-4} \times 10^2 = \dfrac{1}{10^4} \times 10^2 = \dfrac{10 \times 10}{10 \times 10 \times 10 \times 10}$

$= \dfrac{1}{10 \times 10} = 10^{-2}$

● $5^{-3} \times 5^{-4} = \dfrac{1}{5^3} \times \dfrac{1}{5^4} = \dfrac{1}{5^3 \times 5^4} = \dfrac{1}{5^7} = 5^{-7}$

● $(3^2)^{-3} = \dfrac{1}{(3^2)^3} = \dfrac{1}{3^6} = 3^{-6}$

● Discuss how 8^5 can be written as a power of 2.
$(8^5 = (2^3)^5 = 2^{15})$

● What are p and q in this?
$9 \times 15 = 3^p \times 5^q$
$(9 \times 15 = 3 \times 3 \times 3 \times 5 = 3^3 \times 5^1;$
so $p = 3$ and $q = 1)$

INDIVIDUAL WORK

Students work through the rest of the classwork sheet.

Review

Mark any classwork and review the laws of indices and how they are applied.

ANSWERS TO THE CLASSWORK SHEET

Part 1

1 (a) 2^8 (b) 3^5 (c) 5^3 (d) 6^{12}

2 (a) 27 (b) 5

3 (a) $7^3 \times 7^4 \div 7 = 7^6$ (b) $2^7 \times 2^3 \div 2^9 = 2$

Part 2

1 (a) 3^{-1} (b) 5^0 (c) 7^1 (d) 8^{-5}

2 (a) $9^{-2} \times 9^{-4} = 9^{-6}$ (b) $6^3 \div 6^{-2} = 6^5$ (c) $5^4 \times 5^{-6} = 5^{-2}$
(d) $4^{-5} \div 4^4 = 4^{-9}$ (e) $7^2 \div 7^{-4} = 7^6$ (f) $11^3 \div 11^7 = 11^{-4}$

3 (a) 3 (b) 7 (c) 5 (d) −2

4 (a) (i) 3^3 (ii) 3^4 (iii) 3^{12}
(b) (i) 5^3 (ii) 5^6 (iii) 5^{-2}

5 (a) $p = 2, q = 2$ (b) $p = 3, q = 1$ (c) $p = 2, q = -1$
(d) $p = 8, q = 4$ $(2^7 \times 3^5 - 2^7 \times 3^4 = 2^7 \times 3^4(3 - 1)$
$= 2^7 \times 3^4 \times 2 = 2^8 \times 3^4)$
(e) $p = 7, q = 0$ $(2^7 \times 9 - 2^{10} = 2^7(9 - 2^3) = 2^7)$

HOMEWORK

Page
108

HOMEWORK
ANSWERS

Page
137

33 Using indices

Do not use a calculator

Part 1

1 Write each of these as a single power.

(a) $2^3 \times 2^5$ (b) $3^4 \times 3$ (c) $5^6 \div 5^3$ (d) $(6^3)^4$

2 Find the value of each of these, as a whole number.

(a) $(3^3)^2 \times 3^5 \div 3^8$ (b) $5^5 \times 5^4 \div 5^7 \div 5$

3 In each of these one digit has been replaced by *. Copy each part, putting back the digit.

(a) $7^3 \times 7^4 \div 7 = 7^*$ (b) $2^7 \times 2^* \div 2^9 = 2$

Part 2

1 Write each of these as a single power.

(a) $3^7 \div 3^8$ (b) $5^4 \times 5^{-4}$ (c) $7^4 \times 7^{-3}$ (d) $8^{-2} \times 8^{-3}$

2 In each of these one digit has been replaced by a star. Copy each part, putting back the digit.

(a) $9^{-2} \times 9^{-4} = 9^*$ (b) $6^3 \div 6^{-2} = 6^*$

(c) $5^4 \times 5^* = 5^{-2}$ (d) $4^{-5} \div 4^* = 4^{-9}$

(e) $7^2 \div 7^* = 7^6$ (f) $11^3 \div 11^* = 11^{-4}$

3 Find the value of x in each of these.

(a) $3^x = 27$ (b) $x^2 = 49$

(c) $3 \times 2^x = 96$ (d) $18 \times 3^x = 2$

4 (a) Write each of these numbers as a power of 3.

(i) 27   (ii) 9^2 (iii) 9^6

(b) Write each of these numbers as a power of 5.

(i) 125   (ii) 25^3 (iii) 0.04

5 What are p and q in each of these expressions?

(a) $6^2 = 2^p \times 3^q$

(b) $21^3 \div 7^2 = 3^p \times 7^q$

(c) $15^2 \div 5^3 = 3^p \times 5^q$

(d) $2^7 \times 3^5 - 2^7 \times 3^4 = 2^p \times 3^q$

(e) $2^7 \times 9 - 2^{10} = 2^p \times 3^q$

33 Using indices

 **Do not use a calculator**

1 Write each of these as a single power.
  (a) $3^2 \times 3^4$ **(b)** $5^5 \times 5$
  (c) $6^7 \div 6^4$ **(d)** $(7^4)^3$

2 Write each of these as a single power.
  (a) $2^8 \div 2^7$ **(b)** $3^3 \div 3^5$
  (c) $5^4 \times 5^{-2}$ **(d)** $7^3 \times 7^{-6}$

3 Find the value of each of these, as a whole number or as a decimal.
  (a) $7^3 \times 7^4 \div 7^5$ **(b)** $\dfrac{2^8 \times 2^6}{2^{11} \times 2^5}$

4 In each of these one digit has been replaced by *. Copy each part, putting back the digit.
  (a) $3^2 \div 3^3 \times 3^4 = 3^*$
  (b) $5^2 \times 5^3 \times 5^4 = 5^*$
  (c) $5^{-2} \times 5^{-3} = 5^*$
  (d) $3^5 \times 3^* \times 3^{-4} = 3^{-3}$

5 Find the value of x in each of these.
  (a) $2^x = 32$ **(b)** $x^4 = 81$
  (c) $2 \times 3^x = 54$ **(d)** $80 \times 2^x = 10$

6 Find the value of y in each of these.
  (a) $9 \times 27 = 3^y$ **(b)** $125 \times 5^4 = 5^y$
  (c) $(7^4)^y = 7^{12}$ **(d)** $(5^y)^{-4} = 5^8$

7 Find the values of a and b in each of these.
  (a) $15^5 = 3^a \times 5^b$
  (b) $8^2 \times 9^3 = 2^a \times 3^b$
  (c) $12^5 \div 8^6 = 2^a \times 3^b$

34 Standard form

LESSON OBJECTIVES

● Use standard index form expressed in conventional notation

● Convert between ordinary and standard index form representations

● Order numbers expressed in standard index form

WORKING INTERACTIVELY

● Use calculators. Ask students to work out
6.7×10, 6.7×100, 6.7×1000, and so on
until the answer goes into standard form. Discuss
what this means and explain that we *write* 6.7×10^9,
and so on, and point out the link with rules of indices
met in lesson 33.

● Work these out, using a calculator, and interpret the
answers. Which are exact answers and which are not?
$36\,578 \times 56\,342$ ($= 2\,060\,877\,676$, or may be in
standard form with some calculators)
$987\,654\,321 \times 123\,456\,789$ ($= 1.219\,326\,311 \times 10^{17}$)

● Work out, using a calculator,
$6.7 \div 10$, $6.7 \div 100$, $6.7 \div 1000$, and so on
until the answer goes into standard form. Discuss, and
explain that 6.7×10^{-9} means 6.7 divided by 10^9
(because $10^{-9} = \frac{1}{10^9}$, as explained in lesson 33).

● Work these out, using a calculator, and interpret the
answers
$0.0045 \times 0.000\,67$ ($= 0.000\,003\,015$ or 3.015×10^{-6})
$0.000\,012\,6 \times 0.000\,003\,84$ ($= 4.8384 \times 10^{-11}$)

● Discuss converting between the two forms, using
these examples:

5321	($= 5.321 \times 10^3$)
4.36×10^3	($= 4360$)
643 000	($= 6.43 \times 10^5$)
5.731×10^8	($= 573\,100\,000$)
370 000 000 000	($= 3.7 \times 10^{11}$)
6×10^5	($= 600\,000$)
0.036	($= 3.6 \times 10^{-2}$)
3.78×10^{-3}	($= 0.003\,78$)
0.000 004 75	($= 4.75 \times 10^{-6}$)
1.57×10^{-6}	($= 0.000\,001\,57$)

INDIVIDUAL WORK

Students work through the classwork sheet.

Review

Mark any classwork and review conversion between
the two forms.

ANSWERS TO THE CLASSWORK SHEET

1 (a) 4000   (b) 380   (c) 64 000
   (d) 48.5   (e) 408 000   (f) 87 820 000
   (g) 0.06   (h) 0.0046   (i) 0.000 639
   (j) 0.053 28   (k) 0.000 098 76   (l) 0.48

2 (a) 3.7×10^2 (b) 4.8×10^1 (c) 5.2×10^3
   (d) 3×10^4 (e) 6×10^6 (f) 3.2104×10^7
   (g) 8×10^{-1} (h) 5×10^{-2} (i) 3.29×10^{-4}
   (j) 1.01×10^{-2} (k) 7×10^{-6} (l) 1×10^{-7}

3 9×10^2, 4×10^3, 7×10^3, 8×10^5, 1×10^6

4 7×10^{-5}, 4×10^{-4}, 9×10^{-4}, 6×10^{-3}, 2×10^{-1}

5 3×10^{-3}, 5×10^{-1}, 9×10^{-1}, 8×10^2, 4×10^3

6 4.37×10^{-5}, 5.01×10^{-5}, 9.99×10^{-3}, 8.37×10^2, 2.08×10^4

HOMEWORK

**Page
111**

**HOMEWORK
ANSWERS
Page
137**

34 Standard form

 **Do not use a calculator**

1 Rewrite these numbers so that they are *not* in standard form.

(a) 4×10^3 (b) 3.8×10^2 (c) 6.4×10^4 (d) 4.85×10^1

(e) 4.08×10^5 (f) 8.782×10^7 (g) 6×10^{-2} (h) 4.6×10^{-3}

(i) 6.39×10^{-4} (j) 5.328×10^{-2} (k) 9.876×10^{-5} (l) 4.8×10^{-1}

2 Convert these numbers to standard form.

(a) 370   (b) 48   (c) 5200   (d) 30 000

(e) 6 million   (f) 32 104 000   (g) 0.8   (h) 0.05

(i) 0.000 329   (j) 0.0101   (k) 0.000 007   (l) 0.000 000 1

3 Arrange these numbers in order of size, smallest first. Leave them in standard form.

4×10^3 8×10^5 9×10^2 7×10^3 1×10^6

4 Arrange these numbers in order of size, smallest first. Leave them in standard form.

6×10^{-3} 7×10^{-5} 9×10^{-4} 2×10^{-1} 4×10^{-4}

5 Arrange these numbers in order of size, smallest first. Leave them in standard form.

4×10^3 9×10^{-1} 8×10^2 3×10^{-3} 5×10^{-1}

6 Arrange these numbers in order of size, smallest first. Leave them in standard form.

4.37×10^{-5} 9.99×10^{-3} 2.08×10^4 8.37×10^2 5.01×10^{-5}

34 Standard form

Do not use a calculator

1 Rewrite these numbers so that they are *not* in standard form.

(a) 2.35×10^4 (b) 3.576×10^6 (c) 2.431×10^5

(d) 4.2356×10^{12} (e) 6.38×10^{15} (f) 6.41×10^{-4}

(g) 2.538×10^{-6} (h) 1.054×10^{-5} (i) 7.52×10^{-8}

2 Rewrite these numbers in standard form.

(a) 6462   (b) 43 200   (c) 342 000 000

(d) 4 531 200   (e) 0.000 32   (f) 234 000 000 000 000

(g) 0.000 072 3   (h) 0.000 023 7   (i) 0.0081

3 Write these numbers in standard form.

(a) Four thousand   (b) Seven hundred

(c) Six million   (d) Twelve-and-a-half million

4 Place these numbers in order, starting with the smallest. Leave them in standard form.

3.467×10^8 9.935×10^6 4.62×10^8

1.1×10^{11} 3.5×10^8 6.9312×10^9

5 Place these numbers in order, starting with the smallest. Leave them in the form in which they are given.

9.9×10^{-3} 5.23×10^{-1} 0.389

1.42×10^2 4.0005   0.58

3.72×10^{-2} 0   1

35 Standard form with a calculator

LESSON OBJECTIVES

● Calculate with standard index form

● Enter numbers into a calculator using standard index form

● Use standard index form expressed in conventional notation and on a calculator display

---

WORKING INTERACTIVELY

Students need to be able to key in numbers in standard form on their calculators (for example, using the $\boxed{\text{EE}}$ or $\boxed{\text{EXP}}$ button), to perform calculations on such numbers and to interpret the answers.

Examples:

$5.7 \times 10^9 + 3.65 \times 10^{12}$
$\qquad$ ($= 3.6557 \times 10^{12}$ or 3.7×10^{12} to 2 s.f.)

$3.68 \times 10^{13} - 2.775 \times 10^{11}$
$\qquad$ ($= 3.652\ 25 \times 10^{13}$ or 3.65×10^{13} to 3 s.f.)

$8.9 \times 10^5 \times 7.86 \times 10^{12}$
$\qquad$ ($= 6.9954 \times 10^{18}$ or 7.0×10^{18} to 2 s.f.)

$(4.93 \times 10^5)^2$
$\qquad$ ($= 2.430\ 49 \times 10^{11}$ or 2.43×10^{11} to 3 s.f.)

$\overline{\sqrt{9.45 \times 10^7}}$

$\qquad$ ($= 9721.11$ or 9.72×10^3 to 3 s.f.)

INDIVIDUAL WORK (10 MINUTES)

Students work through *Part 1* of the classwork sheet.

WORKING INTERACTIVELY

Extend to calculations involving negative exponents. On most calculators, use the $\boxed{\pm}$ key after the $\boxed{\text{EXP}}$ key. For example, 4.9×10^{-7} is keyed as $\boxed{4}\,\boxed{.}\,\boxed{9}\,\boxed{\text{EXP}}\,\boxed{\pm}\,\boxed{7}$

Examples:
$3.650 \times 10^{-8} + 4.05 \times 10^{-11} = 3.654 \times 10^{-8}$
$8.76 \times 10^{-3} \div 2.45 \times 10^{-7} = 35\ 755$ or 3.58×10^4
(are students surprised by the size of this answer?)

INDIVIDUAL WORK

Students work through *Part 2* of the classwork sheet.

WORKING INTERACTIVELY

Put standard form into context. It is needed for real calculations, particularly in contexts where very large or very small numbers are involved. Some of the questions from *Part 3* of the classwork sheet could be done on the board.

INDIVIDUAL WORK

Students work through the rest of the classwork sheet.

Review

Mark any classwork and review strategies for using students' calculators.

ANSWERS TO THE CLASSWORK SHEET

Part 1

1 8.75×10^5	**2** 4.97×10^{13}	**3** 7.23×10^{11}
4 2.43×10^6	**5** 2.43×10^9	**6** 3.24×10^{15}
7 1.49×10^2	**8** 6.39×10^1	**9** 1.59×10^6
10 1.35×10^{-4}	**11** -1.48×10^5	**12** 5.87×10^1
13 2.41×10^4	**14** 8.68×10^3	

Part 2

1 2.72×10^{-4}	**2** 2.22×10^{-1}	**3** 3.38×10^{-2}
4 5.24×10^1	**5** -1.34×10^{-3}	**6** 9.08×10^4
7 3.13×10^4	**8** 2.79×10^{-7}	**9** 8.02×10^{-19}
10 6.44×10^{-3}		

Part 3

1 5.900×10^9

2 1.496×10^8 km $\div$ 300 000 km per second $= 500$ seconds (to a sensible degree of accuracy) or just over 8 minutes

3 4.008×10^{-26} kg

4 1.91×10^{-28} kg

HOMEWORK

Page
115

HOMEWORK
ANSWERS
Page
137

35 Standard form with a calculator

You need a calculator

Part 1

Carry out each of these calculations and write the answer in standard form. Give all your answers correct to 3 significant figures.

1 $(3.07 \times 10^2) \times (2.85 \times 10^3)$

2 $(6.73 \times 10^5) \times (7.39 \times 10^7)$

3 $137 \times (5.28 \times 10^9)$

4 429×5673

5 $(4.93 \times 10^4)^2$

6 $(1.48 \times 10^5)^3$

7 $(3.87 \times 10^4) \div (2.59 \times 10^2)$

8 $(4.38 \times 10^9) \div (6.85 \times 10^7)$

9 $(1.34 \times 10^6) + (2.54 \times 10^5)$

10 $(7.29 \times 10^2) \div (5.41 \times 10^6)$

11 $(4.89 \times 10^5) - (6.37 \times 10^5)$

12 $\sqrt{3.45 \times 10^3}$

13 $\sqrt{(4.37 \times 10^4) + (5.83 \times 10^8)}$

14 $\dfrac{(4.38 \times 10^7) + (6.27 \times 10^9)}{7.27 \times 10^5}$

Part 2

Carry out each of these calculations and write the answer in standard form. Give all your answers correct to 3 significant figures.

1 $(4.27 \times 10^{-3}) \times (6.37 \times 10^{-2})$

2 $(5.19 \times 10^{-5}) \times (4.28 \times 10^3)$

3 $(5.39 \times 10^{-7}) \times (6.28 \times 10^4)$

4 $(6.23 \times 10^{-6}) \times (8.41 \times 10^6)$

5 $(2.79 \times 10^{-5}) - (1.37 \times 10^{-3})$

6 $(5.79 \times 10^{-4}) \div (6.38 \times 10^{-9})$

7 $(3.13 \times 10^4) + (4.17 \times 10^{-8})$

8 $(5.28 \times 10^{-4})^2$

9 $(9.29 \times 10^{-7})^3$

10 $\sqrt{4.15 \times 10^{-5}}$

Part 3

Give the answers to these questions in standard form. Give all your answers to a sensible degree of accuracy.

1 The average distance of the Earth from the Sun is 1.496×10^8 km.

The average distance of the planet Pluto from the Sun is 39.44 times that of the Earth.

What is the average distance of Pluto from the Sun in kilometres?

2 The speed of light is 300 000 km per second. Use the information given in question 1 to calculate the time taken for the Sun's light to reach the Earth.

3 The mass of an atom of calcium is 40.08 daltons.

Given that 1 dalton = 10^{-27} kg, find the mass of an atom of calcium in kilograms, correct to 3 significant figures.

4 The sub-atomic particle called a muon has a mass equivalent of 106 MeV (million electron volts). 1 MeV = 1.8×10^{-30} kg.

Find the mass of a muon in kilograms.

35

Standard form with a calculator

You need a calculator

> Give the answers to all of these questions in standard form.

1 Calculate these, giving each answer correct to 3 significant figures.
  (a) $(3.4 \times 10^4) \times (5.7 \times 10^6)$

  (b) $(3.4 \times 10^7) \div (1.5 \times 10^3)$

  (c) $(6.28 \times 10^{-4}) \times (1.32 \times 10^9)$

  (d) $(6.53 \times 10^{-4}) \times (9.403 \times 10^{-5})$

  (e) $(3.67 \times 10^4) \div (8.241 \times 10^{13})$

  (f) $(6.02 \times 10^{-11}) \times (2.789 \times 10^5)$

  (g) $(2.6 \times 10^{-3}) \div (1.3 \times 10^{11})$

  (h) $(5.6 \times 10^{-4}) \div (3.46 \times 10^{-19})$

  (i) $(7.52 \times 10^7) + (4.6 \times 10^4)$

  (j) $(7.52 \times 10^7) - (4.6 \times 10^4)$

  (k) $(7.4 \times 10^{-3}) \div (8.32 \times 10^{-12})$

  (l) $(4.65 \times 10^5) \div (8.421 \times 10^{-2})$

2 How many seconds have you been alive?

3 There are approximately 5.7×10^7 people living in Great Britain. On average, each person uses 20 litres of water per day.
  (a) How many litres of water are used throughout Great Britain each day?

  (b) How many litres of water are used in Great Britain each year?

Give your answers in standard form.

4 Light takes about 43 minutes and 15 seconds to reach the planet Jupiter from the Sun.

Light travels at approximately 299 800 kilometres per second.

Calculate, correct to 2 significant figures, the distance from the Sun to Jupiter.

5 The Moon is approximately 4×10^5 km from the Earth. The height of a standard drinks can is about 140 mm.
  (a) How many empty drinks cans would need to be placed end to end to reach from the Earth to the Moon?

  (b) Using the data in question 3, how many empty cans would each person in Britain need to collect, on average, in order to have enough cans to reach from the Earth to the Moon?

36 Standard form without a calculator

LESSON OBJECTIVES

● Use index laws to calculate with standard index form

WORKING INTERACTIVELY

Discuss how these can be worked out without a calculator.

● $(1.2 \times 10^3) \times 4$ This is 4.8×10^3, because $1.2 \times 4 = 4.8$

● $(6.3 \times 10^4) \times 2$ This is 1.26×10^5, because $6.3 \times 2 = 12.6$ and you then adjust to standard form.

● $(4.5 \times 10^5) \times (3 \times 10^6)$ This is $4.5 \times 3 \times 10^5 \times 10^6$ $= 13.5 \times 10^{11} = 1.35 \times 10^{12}$

● $(6 \times 10^3)^2$ This is $6 \times 6 \times 10^3 \times 10^3$ $= 36 \times 10^6 = 3.6 \times 10^7$

● $(8 \times 10^7) \div (2 \times 10^2)$ This is 4×10^5, because $8 \div 2 = 4$

● $(2 \times 10^3) \div (8 \times 10^7)$ This is $(2 \div 8) \times 10^3 \div 10^7$ $= 0.25 \times 10^{-4}$, which needs adjusting to 2.5×10^{-5}

INDIVIDUAL WORK

Students work through *Part 1* of the classwork sheet.

WORKING INTERACTIVELY

Discuss how these can be worked out without a calculator.

● $2.3 \times 10^5 + 3.5 \times 10^5 = (2.3 + 3.5) \times 10^5 = 5.8 \times 10^5$

● $4.7 \times 10^3 + 7.5 \times 10^3 = (4.7 + 7.5) \times 10^3$ $= 12.2 \times 10^3 = 1.22 \times 10^4$

● $3.4 \times 10^6 + 8.1 \times 10^5 = (34 + 8.1) \times 10^5$ $= 42.1 \times 10^5 = 4.21 \times 10^6$

● $4.7 \times 10^8 - 2.9 \times 10^8 = (4.7 - 2.9) \times 10^8 = 1.8 \times 10^8$

● $3.6 \times 10^7 - 7.9 \times 10^5 = (360 - 7.9) \times 10^5$ $= 352.1 \times 10^5 = 3.521 \times 10^7$

INDIVIDUAL WORK

Students work through *Part 2* of the classwork sheet.

WORKING INTERACTIVELY

These questions are more difficult and you may only want to tackle them with some groups.

Discuss how these can be worked out without a calculator.

● $\sqrt{9 \times 10^6} = \sqrt{9} \times 10^3 = 3 \times 10^3$

● $\sqrt{2.5 \times 10^9} = \sqrt{25 \times 10^8} = \sqrt{25} \times 10^4 = 5 \times 10^4$

● $(1.2 \times 10^3) \times (6 \times 10^{-5})$ This is 7.2×10^{-2}

● $(6.3 \times 10^4) \times (3 \times 10^{-7})$ This is 18.9×10^{-3}, which needs adjusting to 1.89×10^{-2}

● $(4.2 \times 10^4) \div (1.4 \times 10^{-6})$ This is $(4.2 \div 1.4) \times 10^{10} = 3 \times 10^{10}$

● $(1.3 \times 10^{-7}) \div (6.5 \times 10^{-4})$ This is $(1.3 \div 6.5) \times 10^{-3} = \frac{1}{5} \times 10^{-3}$ $= 0.2 \times 10^{-3} = 2 \times 10^{-4}$

INDIVIDUAL WORK

Students work through the rest of the classwork sheet.

Review

Mark any classwork and review strategies.

ANSWERS TO THE CLASSWORK SHEET

Part 1

1 4.5×10^5 **2** 1.46×10^4 **3** 1.2×10^6

4 2.6×10^{11} **5** 9×10^8 **6** 4.9×10^{13}

7 3×10^3 **8** 5×10^3 **9** 4.8×10^2

10 2.5×10^2

Part 2

1 7.97×10^7 **2** 1.217×10^5 **3** 7.802×10^6

4 2.2463×10^9 **5** 1.76×10^5 **6** 4.872×10^8

Part 3

1 2×10^4 **2** 7×10^3 **3** 4.8×10^{-2}

4 2.52×10^{-8} **5** 1.2×10^{-2} **6** 5×10^7

HOMEWORK

Page
118

HOMEWORK
ANSWERS
Page
137

36 Standard form without a calculator

 **Do not use a calculator**

Part 1

Carry out each of these calculations and write the *exact* answer in standard form.

1 $(1.5 \times 10^5) \times 3$

2 $(7.3 \times 10^3) \times 2$

3 $(4 \times 10^3) \times (3 \times 10^2)$

4 $(6.5 \times 10^4) \times (4 \times 10^6)$

5 $(3 \times 10^4)^2$

6 $(7 \times 10^6)^2$

7 $(9 \times 10^8) \div (3 \times 10^5)$

8 $(2 \times 10^6) \div (4 \times 10^2)$

9 $(2.4 \times 10^5) \div (5 \times 10^2)$

10 $(7 \times 10^5) \div (2.8 \times 10^3)$

Part 2

Carry out each of these calculations and write the *exact* answer in standard form.

1 $4.23 \times 10^7 + 3.74 \times 10^7$

2 $5.83 \times 10^4 + 6.34 \times 10^4$

3 $6.97 \times 10^6 + 8.32 \times 10^5$

4 $2.16 \times 10^9 + 8.63 \times 10^7$

5 $6.32 \times 10^5 - 4.56 \times 10^5$

6 $5.81 \times 10^8 - 9.38 \times 10^7$

Part 3

Carry out each of these calculations and write the *exact* answer in standard form.

1 $\sqrt{4 \times 10^8}$

2 $\sqrt{4.9 \times 10^7}$

3 $(1.6 \times 10^4) \times (3 \times 10^{-6})$

4 $(8.4 \times 10^{-3}) \times (3 \times 10^{-6})$

5 $(7.2 \times 10^{-5}) \div (6 \times 10^{-3})$

6 $(2.4 \times 10^3) \div (4.8 \times 10^{-5})$

36 Standard form without a calculator

 **Do not use a calculator**

Carry out each of these calculations and write the *exact* answer in standard form.

1 $(2.5 \times 10^7) \times 3$

2 $(3.5 \times 10^5) \times 4$

3 $(4.1 \times 10^8) \times 7$

4 $(9 \times 10^4) \times (8 \times 10^5)$

5 $(4.3 \times 10^3) \times (5 \times 10^2)$

6 $(2 \times 10^5)^2$

7 $(9 \times 10^3)^2$

8 $(6 \times 10^7) \div (2 \times 10^4)$

9 $(4 \times 10^9) \div (8 \times 10^5)$

10 $(3.6 \times 10^7) \div (5 \times 10^2)$

11 $(8 \times 10^{10}) \div (1.6 \times 10^5)$

12 $(2.7 \times 10^7) \div (3.6 \times 10^4)$

13 $7.01 \times 10^9 + 2.49 \times 10^9$

14 $6.91 \times 10^6 - 4.86 \times 10^6$

15 $6.91 \times 10^6 + 4.86 \times 10^6$

16 $4.64 \times 10^7 + 5.75 \times 10^6$

17 $8.01 \times 10^{11} - 9.05 \times 10^9$

18 $\sqrt{6.4 \times 10^7}$

19 $(1.8 \times 10^6) \times (2 \times 10^{-9})$

20 $(2.8 \times 10^{-4}) \div (4 \times 10^{-7})$

37 Adding and subtracting simple fractions

LESSON OBJECTIVES

● Add and subtract simple fractions by writing them with a common denominator

WORKING INTERACTIVELY

● Start with examples where the denominators are the same: mix addition and subtraction examples, e.g.

$\frac{1}{5} + \frac{2}{5}$ (Stress similarity with algebra: 1 fifth + 2 fifths = 3 fifths and $1x + 2x = 3x$)

$\frac{5}{8} - \frac{1}{8}$ $\left(\frac{4}{8} = \frac{1}{2}\right.$ – remind students about putting fractions in simplest form$\left.\right)$

$\frac{3}{10} - \frac{1}{10}$ $\left(\frac{2}{10} = \frac{1}{5}\right)$

$\frac{3}{5} + \frac{4}{5}$ $\left(= \frac{7}{5} = 1\frac{2}{5}\right.$ if we change the **simple fraction** to a **mixed number**$\left.\right)$

● Ask students to suggest further examples to do on the board. They may well suggest one where the fraction is not in its simplest form. This $\left(\text{e.g. } \frac{2}{8} + \frac{3}{8}\right)$ could be used as a way into the next section.

● What about $\frac{1}{4} + \frac{3}{8}$?
Remind students about the work done on ordering fractions, when you have to make the denominators the same. You do the same thing here.

So $\frac{1}{4} + \frac{3}{8} = \frac{2}{8} + \frac{3}{8} = \frac{5}{8}$

● Further examples of the same type to do together:

$\frac{1}{3} + \frac{1}{6}$ $\left(= \frac{3}{6} = \frac{1}{2}\right)$

$\frac{4}{5} - \frac{1}{10}$ $\left(= \frac{7}{10}\right)$

$\frac{7}{12} + \frac{1}{3}$ $\left(= \frac{11}{12}\right)$

● Discuss more difficult examples:

$\frac{2}{3} + \frac{1}{4}$ $\left(= \frac{11}{12}\right)$

$\frac{1}{6} + \frac{2}{9}$ $\left(= \frac{7}{18}\right)$

$\frac{2}{3} - \frac{5}{8}$ $\left(= \frac{1}{24}\right)$

$\frac{4}{5} - \frac{3}{4}$ $\left(= \frac{1}{20}\right)$

$1 - \frac{3}{4}$ $\left(= \frac{1}{4}\right)$

$2\frac{1}{2} + \frac{1}{4}$ $\left(= 2\frac{3}{4}\right)$

$2 - \frac{3}{8}$ $\left(= 1\frac{5}{8}\right)$

INDIVIDUAL WORK

Students work through the classwork sheet.

Review

● You can add and subtract when the denominators are the same:

$\frac{2}{7} + \frac{3}{7} = \frac{5}{7}$

$\frac{3}{5} - \frac{2}{5} = \frac{1}{5}$

● When the denominators are not the same, make them the same by multiplying one or both fractions by a suitable number.

$\frac{3}{5} + \frac{1}{10}$ ⓧ²
$= \frac{6}{10} + \frac{1}{10}$
$= \frac{7}{10}$

$\frac{2}{5} + \frac{1}{4}$ ⓧ⁴ ⓧ⁵
$= \frac{8}{20} + \frac{5}{20}$
$= \frac{13}{20}$

ANSWERS TO THE CLASSWORK SHEET

1 $\frac{5}{8}$	**2** $\frac{1}{12}$	**3** $\frac{1}{2}$	**4** $\frac{1}{10}$
5 $\frac{13}{12} = 1\frac{1}{12}$	**6** $\frac{1}{6}$	**7** 1	**8** 1
9 $\frac{14}{15}$	**10** $\frac{1}{9}$	**11** $\frac{2}{3}$	**12** $\frac{5}{24}$
13 $\frac{13}{18}$	**14** $\frac{1}{8}$	**15** $1\frac{3}{4}$	**16** $4\frac{1}{3}$
17 20	**18** 1500	**19** 16	**20** 800

HOMEWORK

Page
121

HOMEWORK
ANSWERS
Page
137

37 Adding and subtracting simple fractions

 Do not use a calculator

Calculate these.

1 $\dfrac{1}{4} + \dfrac{3}{8}$ **2** $\dfrac{1}{3} - \dfrac{1}{4}$ **3** $\dfrac{1}{3} + \dfrac{1}{6}$

4 $\dfrac{4}{5} - \dfrac{7}{10}$ **5** $\dfrac{1}{3} + \dfrac{3}{4}$ **6** $\dfrac{3}{4} - \dfrac{7}{12}$

7 $\dfrac{1}{5} + \dfrac{4}{5}$ **8** $\dfrac{1}{4} + \dfrac{3}{4}$ **9** $\dfrac{3}{5} + \dfrac{1}{3}$

10 $\dfrac{4}{9} - \dfrac{1}{3}$ **11** $\dfrac{2}{5} + \dfrac{4}{15}$ **12** $\dfrac{7}{8} - \dfrac{2}{3}$

13 $\dfrac{5}{9} + \dfrac{1}{6}$ **14** $1 - \dfrac{7}{8}$ **15** $2 - \dfrac{1}{4}$

16 $5 - \dfrac{2}{3}$

17 At a night club, one-quarter of the people are under 18 and should not be there, because they are under age. One-eighth are over 40 and are to old to be there! There are 50 people between 18 and 40 in the night club. How many under-18s are there?

18 At a school, $\dfrac{3}{5}$ of the students have a school lunch, $\dfrac{1}{10}$ go to the local chip shop and the remaining 150 go home. How many students are in the school?

19 At a party, one-quarter of the guests are men, three-eighths are women and the rest are children. There are 6 children at the party. How many people are at the party altogether?

20 At a school, half the students go home on the school bus, one-quarter walk, one-fifth cycle and the remaining 40 students are collected by car. How many students are in the school?

Lessons in Numeracy (Intermediate) © Longman (an imprint of Pearson Education) 2001

37 Adding and subtracting simple fractions

Do not use a calculator

Calculate these.

1 $\dfrac{1}{4} + \dfrac{5}{8}$ **2** $\dfrac{1}{2} - \dfrac{1}{3}$ **3** $\dfrac{1}{6} + \dfrac{1}{4}$

4 $\dfrac{2}{5} - \dfrac{3}{10}$ **5** $\dfrac{2}{3} + \dfrac{1}{4}$ **6** $\dfrac{3}{4} - \dfrac{5}{12}$

7 $\dfrac{2}{3} + \dfrac{1}{3}$ **8** $\dfrac{3}{4} + \dfrac{1}{2}$ **9** $\dfrac{1}{2} - \dfrac{5}{12}$

10 $\dfrac{5}{6} + \dfrac{3}{4}$ **11** $\dfrac{7}{12} - \dfrac{1}{36}$ **12** $\dfrac{3}{5} + \dfrac{1}{3}$

13 $\dfrac{4}{9} - \dfrac{1}{3}$ **14** $\dfrac{2}{5} + \dfrac{4}{15}$ **15** $\dfrac{5}{8} + \dfrac{2}{3}$

16 $\dfrac{7}{8} - \dfrac{2}{3}$ **17** $\dfrac{5}{9} + \dfrac{1}{6}$ **18** $\dfrac{7}{15} + \dfrac{3}{10}$

19 $\dfrac{11}{15} - \dfrac{7}{10}$ **20** $\dfrac{2}{5} + \dfrac{5}{8}$ **21** $\dfrac{7}{8} - \dfrac{3}{5}$

22 $1 - \dfrac{7}{8}$ **23** $2 - \dfrac{1}{4}$ **24** $5 - \dfrac{2}{3}$

25 $3\dfrac{1}{2} + \dfrac{1}{4}$ **26** $2\dfrac{3}{4} - \dfrac{1}{2}$ **27** $3 - 1\dfrac{1}{4}$

28 $\dfrac{1}{2} + \dfrac{2}{3} + \dfrac{1}{4}$ **29** $\dfrac{7}{8} + \dfrac{1}{4} - \dfrac{1}{2}$ **30** $\dfrac{2}{3} - \dfrac{1}{12} - \dfrac{1}{2}$

Lessons in Numeracy (Intermediate) © Longman (an imprint of Pearson Education) 2001

INTERMEDIATE ● HOMEWORK

37 Adding and subtracting simple fractions

Do not use a calculator

Calculate these.

1 $\dfrac{1}{4} + \dfrac{5}{8}$ **2** $\dfrac{1}{2} - \dfrac{1}{3}$ **3** $\dfrac{1}{6} + \dfrac{1}{4}$

4 $\dfrac{2}{5} - \dfrac{3}{10}$ **5** $\dfrac{2}{3} + \dfrac{1}{4}$ **6** $\dfrac{3}{4} - \dfrac{5}{12}$

7 $\dfrac{2}{3} + \dfrac{1}{3}$ **8** $\dfrac{3}{4} + \dfrac{1}{2}$ **9** $\dfrac{1}{2} - \dfrac{5}{12}$

10 $\dfrac{5}{6} + \dfrac{3}{4}$ **11** $\dfrac{7}{12} - \dfrac{1}{36}$ **12** $\dfrac{3}{5} + \dfrac{1}{3}$

13 $\dfrac{4}{9} - \dfrac{1}{3}$ **14** $\dfrac{2}{5} + \dfrac{4}{15}$ **15** $\dfrac{5}{8} + \dfrac{2}{3}$

16 $\dfrac{7}{8} - \dfrac{2}{3}$ **17** $\dfrac{5}{9} + \dfrac{1}{6}$ **18** $\dfrac{7}{15} + \dfrac{3}{10}$

19 $\dfrac{11}{15} - \dfrac{7}{10}$ **20** $\dfrac{2}{5} + \dfrac{5}{8}$ **21** $\dfrac{7}{8} - \dfrac{3}{5}$

22 $1 - \dfrac{7}{8}$ **23** $2 - \dfrac{1}{4}$ **24** $5 - \dfrac{2}{3}$

25 $3\dfrac{1}{2} + \dfrac{1}{4}$ **26** $2\dfrac{3}{4} - \dfrac{1}{2}$ **27** $3 - 1\dfrac{1}{4}$

28 $\dfrac{1}{2} + \dfrac{2}{3} + \dfrac{1}{4}$ **29** $\dfrac{7}{8} + \dfrac{1}{4} - \dfrac{1}{2}$ **30** $\dfrac{2}{3} - \dfrac{1}{12} - \dfrac{1}{2}$

Lessons in Numeracy (Intermediate) © Longman (an imprint of Pearson Education) 2001

38 Multiplying and dividing simple fractions

WORKING INTERACTIVELY

Multiplying a fraction by an integer

● $3 \times \frac{1}{4}$ can be read as 'three lots of one-quarter' which is $\frac{3}{4}$. This is the same as $\frac{1}{4} \times 3$.

● Similarly, $2 \times \frac{2}{5}$ is 'two lots of two-fifths', or $\frac{2}{5} + \frac{2}{5} = \frac{4}{5}$. This is the same as $\frac{2}{5} \times 2$.

● Further examples:

$$3 \times \frac{1}{5} \quad \left(= \frac{3}{5}\right)$$

$$4 \times \frac{1}{8} \quad \left(= \frac{4}{8} = \frac{1}{2}\right)$$

$$\frac{1}{5} \times 4 \quad \left(= \frac{4}{5}\right)$$

$$\frac{3}{5} \times 2 \quad \left(= \frac{6}{5} = 1\frac{1}{5}\right)$$

Multiplying a fraction by a unit fraction

● $\frac{1}{2} \times \frac{2}{5}$ can be read as 'half of two-fifths' which is $\frac{1}{5}$.

Similarly:

$$\frac{1}{3} \times \frac{3}{4} \qquad \left(= \frac{1}{4}\right)$$

$$\frac{1}{2} \times \frac{4}{5} \qquad \left(= \frac{2}{5}\right)$$

$$\frac{1}{4} \times \frac{8}{9} \qquad \left(= \frac{2}{9}\right)$$

$$\frac{3}{5} \times \frac{1}{3} \qquad \left(= \frac{1}{3} \times \frac{3}{5} = \frac{1}{5}\right)$$

● What about $\frac{1}{2} \times \frac{1}{4}$? This can be read as 'half of one-quarter' which is $\frac{1}{8}$.

$$\frac{1}{2} \times \frac{3}{4} = \frac{3}{8} \quad \text{(compare with previous example)}$$

● Other examples:

$$\frac{1}{3} \times \frac{1}{4} \qquad \left(= \frac{1}{12}\right)$$

$$\frac{1}{4} \times \frac{1}{5} \qquad \left(= \frac{1}{20}\right)$$

$$\frac{1}{4} \times \frac{3}{5} \qquad \left(= \frac{3}{20}\right)$$

$$\frac{1}{6} \times \frac{1}{4} \qquad \left(= \frac{1}{24}\right)$$

Multiplying two simple fractions

By now, students may have noticed that the answers can be obtained by multiplying the numerators and the denominators.

$$\frac{1}{4} \times \frac{3}{5} = \frac{1 \times 3}{4 \times 5} = \frac{3}{20}$$

$$\frac{2}{3} \times \frac{1}{4} = \frac{2 \times 1}{3 \times 4} = \frac{2}{12} = \frac{1}{6}$$

$$\frac{5}{8} \times \frac{1}{2} = \frac{5 \times 1}{8 \times 3} = \frac{5}{16}$$

$$\frac{3}{8} \times \frac{2}{3} = \frac{6}{24} = \frac{1}{4}$$

INDIVIDUAL WORK

Students work through *Part 1* of the classwork sheet.

WORKING INTERACTIVELY

Dividing a fraction by an integer

● $\frac{3}{4} \div 3$ is clearly $\frac{1}{4}$

$$\frac{6}{7} \div 3 = \frac{2}{7}$$

● $\frac{1}{4} \div 2$ can be read as 'half of $\frac{1}{4}$', exactly like $\frac{1}{2} \times \frac{1}{4}$ discussed earlier.

● For examples like $\frac{3}{4} \div 6$, change to $\frac{6}{8} \div 6$; so the answer is $\frac{1}{8}$.

● Other examples:

$$\frac{2}{3} \div 4 \qquad \left(= \frac{4}{6} \div 4 = \frac{1}{6}\right)$$

$$\frac{5}{8} \div 15 \qquad \left(= \frac{15}{24} \div 15 = \frac{1}{24}\right)$$

$$\frac{3}{8} \div 5 \qquad \left(= \frac{15}{40} \div 5 = \frac{3}{40}\right)$$

$$\frac{7}{10} \div 4 \qquad \left(= \frac{28}{40} \div 4 = \frac{7}{40}\right)$$

Dividing an integer by a fraction

- Discuss questions like these:

  How many halves in a whole one?
  So $1 \div \frac{1}{2} = 2$

  How many thirds in a whole one?
  So $1 \div \frac{1}{3} = 3$

  How many quarters in 2?
  So $2 \div \frac{1}{4} = 8$

  How many quarters in 3?
  So $3 \div \frac{1}{4} = 12$

  How many three-quarters are there in 3?
  So $3 \div \frac{3}{4} = 4$

  How many three-quarters are there in 6?
  So $6 \div \frac{3}{4} = 8$

Dividing a fraction by a fraction

- Discuss questions like these:

  What is $\frac{3}{7} \div \frac{6}{7}$? Either $\frac{3}{7} \div \frac{6}{7} = 3 \div 6 = \frac{1}{2}$

  or $\frac{3}{7} \div \frac{6}{7} = \frac{3}{7} \times \frac{7}{6} = \frac{3}{6} = \frac{1}{2}$

  What is $\frac{3}{4} \div \frac{2}{3}$? Either $\frac{3}{4} \div \frac{2}{3} = \frac{9}{12} \div \frac{8}{12} = 9 \div 8 = 1\frac{1}{8}$

  or $\frac{3}{4} \div \frac{2}{3} = \frac{3}{4} \times \frac{3}{2} = \frac{9}{8} = 1\frac{1}{8}$

INDIVIDUAL WORK

Students work through the rest of the classwork sheet.

Review

Emphasis is on 'common sense' understanding of the
fractions and use of vocabulary.
Some students will find it helpful to remember rules
for multiplying and dividing fractions.

ANSWERS TO THE CLASSWORK SHEET

Part 1

1 $\frac{5}{6}$	**2** $\frac{2}{5}$	**3** $\frac{4}{7}$	**4** $\frac{3}{4}$	**5** $\frac{5}{8}$	**6** $\frac{4}{9}$
7 $\frac{1}{7}$	**8** $\frac{1}{8}$	**9** $\frac{2}{9}$	**10** $\frac{3}{10}$	**11** $\frac{4}{9}$	**12** $\frac{2}{7}$
13 $\frac{4}{15}$	**14** $\frac{9}{32}$	**15** $\frac{8}{25}$	**16** $\frac{1}{2}$	**17** $\frac{1}{2}$	**18** $\frac{8}{27}$
19 $\frac{7}{12}$	**20** $\frac{3}{8}$				

Part 2

1 $\frac{1}{5}$	**2** $\frac{1}{7}$	**3** $\frac{2}{9}$	**4** $\frac{1}{6}$	**5** $\frac{1}{15}$	**6** $\frac{1}{20}$
7 4	**8** 6	**9** 20	**10** 3	**11** 9	**12** 12
13 2	**14** $\frac{1}{3}$	**15** $1\frac{1}{2}$	**16** $1\frac{1}{3}$	**17** $\frac{5}{6}$	**18** $1\frac{1}{2}$
19 $\frac{9}{10}$	**20** $\frac{9}{20}$				

HOMEWORK
Page
125

HOMEWORK
ANSWERS
Page
137

38 Multiplying and dividing simple fractions

 **Do not use a calculator**

Part 1

Calculate these.

1 $5 \times \frac{1}{6}$ **2** $2 \times \frac{1}{5}$ **3** $4 \times \frac{1}{7}$ **4** $\frac{1}{4} \times 3$ **5** $\frac{1}{8} \times 5$

6 $\frac{1}{9} \times 4$ **7** $\frac{1}{2} \times \frac{2}{7}$ **8** $\frac{1}{3} \times \frac{3}{8}$ **9** $\frac{1}{2} \times \frac{4}{9}$ **10** $\frac{1}{3} \times \frac{9}{10}$

11 $\frac{1}{2} \times \frac{8}{9}$ **12** $\frac{1}{3} \times \frac{6}{7}$ **13** $\frac{2}{3} \times \frac{2}{5}$ **14** $\frac{3}{4} \times \frac{3}{8}$ **15** $\frac{4}{5} \times \frac{2}{5}$

16 $\frac{2}{3} \times \frac{3}{4}$ **17** $\frac{3}{5} \times \frac{5}{6}$ **18** $\frac{2}{3} \times \frac{4}{9}$ **19** $\frac{3}{4} \times \frac{7}{9}$ **20** $\frac{7}{8} \times \frac{3}{7}$

Part 2

Calculate these.

1 $\frac{3}{5} \div 3$ **2** $\frac{2}{7} \div 2$ **3** $\frac{8}{9} \div 4$ **4** $\frac{2}{3} \div 4$ **5** $\frac{1}{5} \div 3$

6 $\frac{1}{4} \div 5$ **7** $1 \div \frac{1}{4}$ **8** $2 \div \frac{1}{3}$ **9** $5 \div \frac{1}{4}$ **10** $2 \div \frac{2}{3}$

11 $6 \div \frac{2}{3}$ **12** $9 \div \frac{3}{4}$ **13** $\frac{4}{5} \div \frac{2}{5}$ **14** $\frac{3}{10} \div \frac{9}{10}$ **15** $\frac{6}{7} \div \frac{4}{7}$

16 $\frac{1}{3} \div \frac{1}{4}$ **17** $\frac{1}{6} \div \frac{1}{5}$ **18** $\frac{5}{6} \div \frac{5}{9}$ **19** $\frac{3}{5} \div \frac{2}{3}$ **20** $\frac{3}{8} \div \frac{5}{6}$

38 Multiplying and dividing simple fractions

Do not use a calculator

Calculate these.

1 $\dfrac{1}{4} \times \dfrac{3}{5}$

2 $\dfrac{1}{3} \times \dfrac{5}{8}$

3 $\dfrac{1}{6} \times \dfrac{1}{4}$

4 $\dfrac{2}{5} \times \dfrac{3}{10}$

5 $\dfrac{2}{3} \times \dfrac{1}{4}$

6 $\dfrac{3}{4} \times \dfrac{5}{12}$

7 $\dfrac{4}{5} \times \dfrac{5}{12}$

8 $\dfrac{5}{16} \times \dfrac{8}{15}$

9 $\dfrac{2}{3} \times \dfrac{3}{4} \times \dfrac{4}{5}$

10 $\dfrac{3}{4} \times \dfrac{4}{5} \times 6$

11 $1 \div \dfrac{1}{8}$

12 $2 \div \dfrac{1}{3}$

13 $2 \div \dfrac{2}{5}$

14 $3 \div \dfrac{1}{4}$

15 $8 \div \dfrac{2}{3}$

16 $\dfrac{4}{5} \div 2$

17 $\dfrac{9}{10} \div 3$

18 $\dfrac{4}{5} \div 8$

19 $\dfrac{3}{4} \div 9$

20 $\dfrac{4}{5} \div \dfrac{2}{5}$

21 $\dfrac{3}{8} \div \dfrac{1}{8}$

22 $\dfrac{5}{9} \div \dfrac{2}{9}$

23 $\dfrac{8}{9} \div \dfrac{2}{3}$

24 $\dfrac{3}{4} \div \dfrac{3}{5}$

25 $\dfrac{2}{3} \div \dfrac{1}{2}$

26 $\dfrac{5}{8} \div \dfrac{1}{4}$

27 $\dfrac{3}{8} \div \dfrac{7}{12}$

28 $\dfrac{1}{5} \div \dfrac{1}{10}$

29 $\dfrac{1}{10} \div \dfrac{1}{5}$

30 $\dfrac{15}{16} \div \dfrac{5}{24}$

Lessons in Numeracy (Intermediate) © Longman (an imprint of Pearson Education) 2001

INTERMEDIATE ● HOMEWORK

38 Multiplying and dividing simple fractions

Do not use a calculator

Calculate these.

1 $\dfrac{1}{4} \times \dfrac{3}{5}$

2 $\dfrac{1}{3} \times \dfrac{5}{8}$

3 $\dfrac{1}{6} \times \dfrac{1}{4}$

4 $\dfrac{2}{5} \times \dfrac{3}{10}$

5 $\dfrac{2}{3} \times \dfrac{1}{4}$

6 $\dfrac{3}{4} \times \dfrac{5}{12}$

7 $\dfrac{4}{5} \times \dfrac{5}{12}$

8 $\dfrac{5}{16} \times \dfrac{8}{15}$

9 $\dfrac{2}{3} \times \dfrac{3}{4} \times \dfrac{4}{5}$

10 $\dfrac{3}{4} \times \dfrac{4}{5} \times 6$

11 $1 \div \dfrac{1}{8}$

12 $2 \div \dfrac{1}{3}$

13 $2 \div \dfrac{2}{5}$

14 $3 \div \dfrac{1}{4}$

15 $8 \div \dfrac{2}{3}$

16 $\dfrac{4}{5} \div 2$

17 $\dfrac{9}{10} \div 3$

18 $\dfrac{4}{5} \div 8$

19 $\dfrac{3}{4} \div 9$

20 $\dfrac{4}{5} \div \dfrac{2}{5}$

21 $\dfrac{3}{8} \div \dfrac{1}{8}$

22 $\dfrac{5}{9} \div \dfrac{2}{9}$

23 $\dfrac{8}{9} \div \dfrac{2}{3}$

24 $\dfrac{3}{4} \div \dfrac{3}{5}$

25 $\dfrac{2}{3} \div \dfrac{1}{2}$

26 $\dfrac{5}{8} \div \dfrac{1}{4}$

27 $\dfrac{3}{8} \div \dfrac{7}{12}$

28 $\dfrac{1}{5} \div \dfrac{1}{10}$

29 $\dfrac{1}{10} \div \dfrac{1}{5}$

30 $\dfrac{15}{16} \div \dfrac{5}{24}$

Lessons in Numeracy (Intermediate) © Longman (an imprint of Pearson Education) 2001

39 The four rules of fractions

> **LESSON OBJECTIVES**
> ● Add, subtract, multiply and divide fractions, including mixed numbers

WORKING INTERACTIVELY

Mixed numbers

$\frac{7}{2}$ means 7 halves and 7 halves is $3\frac{1}{2}$.

● $\frac{7}{2}$ is called a **top-heavy fraction**. $3\frac{1}{2}$ is called a **mixed number**.

● What are these, written as mixed numbers?

$\frac{5}{3}$ $\frac{5}{2}$ $\frac{8}{3}$ $\frac{7}{4}$

● What are these as top-heavy fractions?

$2\frac{1}{4}$ $1\frac{1}{5}$ $3\frac{3}{4}$ $5\frac{2}{3}$

INDIVIDUAL WORK

Students work through *Part 1* of the classwork sheet.

WORKING INTERACTIVELY

Adding and subtracting mixed numbers

● $2\frac{3}{4} + 1\frac{5}{8}$

$= \frac{11}{4} + \frac{13}{8}$

$= \frac{22}{8} + \frac{13}{8}$

$= \frac{35}{8}$

$= 4\frac{3}{8}$

● $5\frac{2}{5} - 3\frac{1}{2}$

$= \frac{27}{5} - \frac{7}{2}$

$= \frac{54}{10} - \frac{35}{10}$

$= \frac{19}{10}$

$= 1\frac{9}{10}$

● This method is suggested (rather than adding or subtracting the whole numbers first) because it works for all four operations: you *always* turn mixed numbers into top-heavy fractions and then proceed as for simple fractions.

INDIVIDUAL WORK

Students work through *Part 2* of the classwork sheet.

WORKING INTERACTIVELY

Multiplying and dividing mixed numbers

● $2\frac{2}{3} \times 4\frac{1}{2}$

$= \frac{8}{3} \times \frac{9}{2}$

$= \frac{8 \times 9}{3 \times 2}$

$= 12$

● $2\frac{3}{5} \times 5$

$= \frac{13}{5} \times 5$

$= 13$

● $1\frac{3}{4} \div 2\frac{1}{3}$

$= \frac{7}{4} \div \frac{7}{3}$

$= \frac{1}{4} \div \frac{1}{3}$ or $\frac{7}{4} \times \frac{3}{7}$

$= \frac{3}{4}$

● $15 \div 3\frac{1}{3}$

$= 15 \div \frac{10}{3}$

$= \frac{45}{3} \div \frac{10}{3}$ or $\frac{15}{1} \times \frac{3}{10}$

$= \frac{45}{10}$

$= 4\frac{1}{2}$

INDIVIDUAL WORK

Students work through the rest of the classwork sheet.

Review

Review key strategies.

ANSWERS TO THE CLASSWORK SHEET

Part 1

1 (a) $2\frac{1}{3}$ **(b)** $5\frac{1}{2}$ **(c)** $5\frac{1}{4}$ **(d)** $2\frac{2}{5}$ **(e)** $1\frac{6}{7}$ **(f)** $2\frac{5}{8}$

2 (a) $\frac{7}{6}$ **(b)** $\frac{16}{5}$ **(c)** $\frac{19}{4}$ **(d)** $\frac{45}{8}$ **(e)** $\frac{9}{7}$ **(f)** $\frac{25}{3}$

Part 2

1 $4\frac{1}{12}$ **2** $7\frac{1}{2}$ **3** $3\frac{3}{8}$ **4** $1\frac{7}{12}$ **5** $4\frac{3}{4}$ **6** $\frac{3}{16}$

Part 3

1 8 **2** $9\frac{3}{4}$ **3** 3 **4** $1\frac{9}{10}$ **5** $2\frac{1}{2}$ **6** $1\frac{1}{3}$

HOMEWORK

Page
128

HOMEWORK
ANSWERS
Page
137

39 The four rules of fractions

INTERMEDIATE ● CLASSWORK

39 The four rules of fractions

Do not use a calculator

Part 1

1 Convert these to mixed numbers.

(a) $\frac{7}{3}$ (b) $\frac{11}{2}$ (c) $\frac{21}{4}$ (d) $\frac{12}{5}$ (e) $\frac{13}{7}$ (f) $\frac{21}{8}$

2 Convert these to top-heavy fractions.

(a) $1\frac{1}{6}$ (b) $3\frac{1}{5}$ (c) $4\frac{3}{4}$ (d) $5\frac{5}{8}$ (e) $1\frac{2}{7}$ (f) $8\frac{1}{3}$

Part 2

Calculate these.

1 $2\frac{3}{4} + 1\frac{1}{3}$ **2** $3\frac{2}{5} + 4\frac{1}{10}$ **3** $5\frac{3}{4} - 2\frac{3}{8}$

4 $5\frac{1}{3} - 3\frac{3}{4}$ **5** $6\frac{1}{12} - 1\frac{1}{3}$ **6** $4\frac{1}{16} - 3\frac{7}{8}$

Part 3

Calculate these.

1 $3\frac{1}{2} \times 2\frac{2}{7}$ **2** $4\frac{1}{3} \times 2\frac{1}{4}$ **3** $2\frac{2}{3} + \frac{8}{9}$

4 $2\frac{3}{8} + 1\frac{1}{4}$ **5** $8\frac{1}{3} + 3\frac{1}{3}$ **6** $2\frac{1}{4} + 1\frac{11}{16}$

39 The four rules of fractions

 Do not use a calculator

Calculate these.

1 $3\frac{2}{3} + 4\frac{3}{4}$

2 $1\frac{3}{10} + 5\frac{1}{5}$

3 $2\frac{5}{6} + 11\frac{1}{3}$

4 $5\frac{1}{2} - 2\frac{1}{6}$

5 $7\frac{1}{8} - 3\frac{5}{8}$

6 $6\frac{1}{4} - 5\frac{1}{3}$

7 $2\frac{3}{4} + 5\frac{1}{3} + 1\frac{11}{12}$

8 $5\frac{1}{4} - 4\frac{1}{3} + 3\frac{1}{2}$

9 $2\frac{1}{3} \times 2\frac{4}{7}$

10 $5\frac{1}{3} \times 2\frac{3}{4}$

11 $3\frac{1}{3} \times \frac{3}{10}$

12 $3\frac{2}{3} \div \frac{11}{12}$

13 $3\frac{5}{6} \div 1\frac{2}{3}$

14 $4\frac{4}{5} \times 1\frac{7}{9}$

15 $1\frac{1}{2} \times 1\frac{1}{4} \div 1\frac{1}{3}$

16 $2\frac{1}{2} \times 1\frac{3}{5} \times 10\frac{1}{2}$

17 A student walks for $\frac{1}{3}$ mile to the bus stop, and then travels $5\frac{3}{4}$ miles by bus to school. What is the total distance travelled to school by this student?

18 To change gallons to litres, you can work out an approximate answer by multiplying the number of gallons by $4\frac{1}{2}$.
Use this approximation to change $7\frac{1}{2}$ gallons to litres.

19 It takes $2\frac{1}{2}$ minutes to swim $3\frac{3}{4}$ lengths of a swimming pool at a constant speed. How long does it take to swim one length of the pool?

20 A 1-litre carton of milk contains the equivalent of $1\frac{3}{4}$ pints. How many pints are the same as $5\frac{1}{2}$ litres?

Lessons in Numeracy (Intermediate) © Longman (an imprint of Pearson Education) 2001

40 Square roots and surds

> **LESSON OBJECTIVES**
> ● Calculate square roots without a calculator
> ● Use surds in exact calculation without a calculator

WORKING INTERACTIVELY

● Recall with students these results:
$\sqrt{4} = 2$, $\sqrt{9} = 3$, $\sqrt{16} = 4$, $\sqrt{25} = 5$, $\sqrt{36} = 6$, ..., $\sqrt{225} = 15$

● Students should be able to see that, for example, $\sqrt{900} = 30$. This can be used to demonstrate a general rule:
$\sqrt{900} = \sqrt{9 \times 100} = \sqrt{9} \times \sqrt{100} = 3 \times 10 = 30$

● This rule can be checked further using examples such as these:
$\sqrt{81} = 9$ and $\sqrt{81} = \sqrt{9 \times 9} = \sqrt{9} \times \sqrt{9} = 3 \times 3 = 9$
$\sqrt{1600} = 40$ and
$\sqrt{1600} = \sqrt{16 \times 100} = \sqrt{16} \times \sqrt{100} = 4 \times 10 = 40$

● Other square roots can be found using this rule. Here are some examples:
$\sqrt{256} = \sqrt{4 \times 64} = \sqrt{4} \times \sqrt{64} = 2 \times 8 = 16$
$\sqrt{1764} = \sqrt{4 \times 441} = \sqrt{4 \times 9 \times 49}$
$= \sqrt{4} \times \sqrt{9} \times \sqrt{49} = 2 \times 3 \times 7 = 42$
(using divisibility rules discussed in lesson 9)
$\sqrt{490\,000} = \sqrt{49} \times \sqrt{100} \times \sqrt{100} = 7 \times 10 \times 10 = 700$
$\sqrt{14\,400} = \sqrt{144} \times \sqrt{100} = 12 \times 10 = 120$

● The same rule can be used to find, for example, $\sqrt{0.16}$.
$\sqrt{0.16} = \sqrt{\frac{16}{100}} = \frac{\sqrt{16}}{\sqrt{100}} = \frac{4}{10} = 0.4$

● Here are some more examples.
$\sqrt{0.09} = \sqrt{\frac{9}{100}} = \frac{\sqrt{9}}{\sqrt{100}} = \frac{3}{10} = 0.3$
$\sqrt{0.0036} = \sqrt{\frac{36}{10\,000}} = \frac{\sqrt{36}}{\sqrt{10\,000}} = \frac{6}{100} = 0.06$

INDIVIDUAL WORK

Students work through *Part 1* of the classwork sheet.

WORKING INTERACTIVELY

● The first half of the lesson was about a rule for multiplying square roots. Point out that there is *no* similar rule for addition or subtraction.

● For example: $\sqrt{4} + \sqrt{9} = 2 + 3 = 5$; but $\sqrt{4 + 9} = \sqrt{13}$, which is *not* equal to 5.
$\sqrt{16} - \sqrt{9} = 4 - 3 = 1$; but $\sqrt{16 - 9} = \sqrt{7}$.

● But you can add or subtract the *same* square roots.
For example: $\sqrt{3} + \sqrt{3} = 2\sqrt{3}$
(We do not usually write $2 \times \sqrt{3}$. Compare with $2x$.)
$4\sqrt{5} + 2\sqrt{5} = 6\sqrt{5}$ (Compare with $4x + 2x = 6x$.)

● Here we are simplifying expressions with square roots, like $\sqrt{3}$ and $\sqrt{5}$, which are *not* exact decimals. Such expressions are often called **surds**.

● Using this, and using the *multiplication* rule, slightly more complicated expressions can be simplified.

● For example:
$\sqrt{8} + \sqrt{2} = \sqrt{4 \times 2} + \sqrt{2} = (\sqrt{4} \times \sqrt{2}) + \sqrt{2} = 2\sqrt{2} + \sqrt{2} = 3\sqrt{2}$
$\sqrt{18} + \sqrt{2} = \sqrt{9 \times 2} + \sqrt{2} = \sqrt{9} \times \sqrt{2} + \sqrt{2} = 3\sqrt{2} + \sqrt{2} = 4\sqrt{2}$
$\sqrt{75} + 2\sqrt{3} = \sqrt{25 \times 3} + 2\sqrt{3} = \sqrt{25} \times \sqrt{3} + 2\sqrt{3}$
$\qquad = 5\sqrt{3} + 2\sqrt{3} = 7\sqrt{3}$
$\sqrt{125} - \sqrt{80} = \sqrt{25 \times 5} - \sqrt{16 \times 5} = 5\sqrt{5} - 4\sqrt{5} = \sqrt{5}$
$\sqrt{8} \times \sqrt{2} = \sqrt{16} = 4$

INDIVIDUAL WORK

Students work through *Part 2* of the classwork sheet.

> ### Review
> Review key strategies:
> ● $ab = \sqrt{a} \times \sqrt{b}$
> ● $\left(\frac{a}{b}\right) = \frac{\sqrt{a}}{\sqrt{b}}$
> ● $(\sqrt{a})^2 = a$
> ● But $\sqrt{a + b} \neq \sqrt{a} + \sqrt{b}$
> and $\sqrt{a - b} \neq \sqrt{a} - \sqrt{b}$
> ● You can add or subtract surds if the square roots are the same:
> $7\sqrt{3} + 4\sqrt{3} = 11\sqrt{3}$
> $7\sqrt{5} - 4\sqrt{5} = 3\sqrt{5}$
> $\sqrt{50} - \sqrt{2} = \sqrt{25 \times 2} - \sqrt{2} = 5\sqrt{2} - \sqrt{2} = 4\sqrt{2}$

ANSWERS TO THE CLASSWORK SHEET

Part 1

1 (a) 8 (b) 5 (c) 20 (d) 60 (e) 70 (f) 900

2 (a) 18 (b) 27 (c) 25 (d) 24 (e) 21 (f) 35

3 (a) 0.1 (b) 0.3 (c) 0.5 (d) 0.07 (e) 0.09 (f) 0.11

Part 2

1 (a) $5\sqrt{3}$ (b) $7\sqrt{5}$ (c) $8\sqrt{7}$ (d) $3\sqrt{2}$ (e) $\sqrt{5}$ (f) $3\sqrt{6}$

2 (a) $3\sqrt{3}$ (b) $5\sqrt{2}$ (c) $4\sqrt{3}$ (d) $\sqrt{2}$ (e) $3\sqrt{3}$ (f) $2\sqrt{5}$

3 (a) $5\sqrt{2}$ (b) $5\sqrt{3}$ (c) $7\sqrt{5}$ (d) $2\sqrt{3}$ (e) $\sqrt{5}$ (f) $2\sqrt{2}$

4 (a) 6 (b) 3 (c) 12 (d) 17

HOMEWORK

Page 132

HOMEWORK ANSWERS Page 137

40 Square roots and surds

Do not use a calculator

Part 1

1 Find the value of these.
   (a) $\sqrt{64}$ (b) $\sqrt{25}$ (c) $\sqrt{400}$
   (d) $\sqrt{3600}$ (e) $\sqrt{4900}$ (f) $\sqrt{810\,000}$

2 Use factorisation rules to help you find the values of these.
   (a) $\sqrt{324}$ (b) $\sqrt{729}$ (c) $\sqrt{625}$
   (d) $\sqrt{576}$ (e) $\sqrt{441}$ (f) $\sqrt{1225}$

3 Find the value of these.
   (a) $\sqrt{0.01}$ (b) $\sqrt{0.09}$ (c) $\sqrt{0.25}$
   (d) $\sqrt{0.0049}$ (e) $\sqrt{0.0081}$ (f) $\sqrt{0.0121}$

Part 2

1 Simplify these.
   (a) $3\sqrt{3} + 2\sqrt{3}$ (b) $\sqrt{5} + 6\sqrt{5}$ (c) $\sqrt{7} + 7\sqrt{7}$
   (d) $8\sqrt{2} - 5\sqrt{2}$ (e) $4\sqrt{5} - 3\sqrt{5}$ (f) $6\sqrt{6} - 3\sqrt{6}$

2 Simplify these.
   (a) $\sqrt{12} + \sqrt{3}$ (b) $\sqrt{32} + \sqrt{2}$ (c) $\sqrt{27} + \sqrt{3}$
   (d) $\sqrt{8} - \sqrt{2}$ (e) $\sqrt{48} - \sqrt{3}$ (f) $\sqrt{45} - \sqrt{5}$

3 Simplify these.
   (a) $\sqrt{8} + \sqrt{18}$ (b) $\sqrt{27} + \sqrt{12}$ (c) $\sqrt{20} + \sqrt{125}$
   (d) $\sqrt{48} - \sqrt{12}$ (e) $\sqrt{80} - \sqrt{45}$ (f) $\sqrt{32} - \sqrt{8}$

4 Simplify these.
   (a) $\sqrt{3} \times \sqrt{12}$ (b) $\sqrt{3} \times \sqrt{3}$ (c) $\sqrt{8} \times \sqrt{18}$
   (d) $\sqrt{17} \times \sqrt{17}$

40 Square roots and surds

Do not use a calculator

1 Find the value of these.

(a) √9　　(b) √49　　(c) √900

(d) √2500　　(e) √12 100　　(f) √40 000

2 Use factorisation rules to help you find the values of these.

(a) √225　　(b) √441　　(c) √1024

(d) √729　　(e) √1296　　(f) √11 025

3 Find the value of these.

(a) √0.04　　(b) √0.36　　(c) √0.16

(d) √0.0025　　(e) √0.0144　　(f) √0.0196

4 Simplify these.

(a) 4√5 + 3√5　　(b) √11 + 4√11　　(c) √10 + 3√10

(d) 7√3 − 3√3　　(e) 8√2 − 7√2　　(f) 9√13 − 5√13 − 4√13

5 Simplify these.

(a) √75 + √3　　(b) √80 + √5　　(c) √125 + √5

(d) √18 − √2　　(e) √75 − √3　　(f) √28 − √7

6 Simplify these.

(a) √20 + √45　　(b) √63 + √28　　(c) √24 + √150

(d) √90 − √40　　(e) √99 − √44　　(f) √175 − √28

7 Simplify these.

(a) √5 × √20　　(b) √7 × √7　　(c) √3 × √48　　(d) √27 × √75

Lessons in Numeracy (Intermediate) © Longman (an imprint of Pearson Education) 2001

INTERMEDIATE ● HOMEWORK

40 Square roots and surds

Do not use a calculator

1 Find the value of these.

(a) √9　　(b) √49　　(c) √900

(d) √2500　　(e) √12 100　　(f) √40 000

2 Use factorisation rules to help you find the values of these.

(a) √225　　(b) √441　　(c) √1024

(d) √729　　(e) √1296　　(f) √11 025

3 Find the value of these.

(a) √0.04　　(b) √0.36　　(c) √0.16

(d) √0.0025　　(e) √0.0144　　(f) √0.0196

4 Simplify these.

(a) 4√5 + 3√5　　(b) √11 + 4√11　　(c) √10 + 3√10

(d) 7√3 − 3√3　　(e) 8√2 − 7√2　　(f) 9√13 − 5√13 − 4√13

5 Simplify these.

(a) √75 + √3　　(b) √80 + √5　　(c) √125 + √5

(d) √18 − √2　　(e) √75 − √3　　(f) √28 − √7

6 Simplify these.

(a) √20 + √45　　(b) √63 + √28　　(c) √24 + √150

(d) √90 − √40　　(e) √99 − √44　　(f) √175 − √28

7 Simplify these.

(a) √5 × √20　　(b) √7 × √7　　(c) √3 × √48　　(d) √27 × √75

Lessons in Numeracy (Intermediate) © Longman (an imprint of Pearson Education) 2001

Answers to Homework

1 Mental strategies for addition and subtraction

1 38, 53, 68, 83, 98, 113, 128, 143, 158, 173
2 1993, 1986, 1979, 1972, 1965, 1958, 1951, 1944, 1937, 1930
3 4961, 4922, 4883, 4844, 4805, 4766, 4727, 4688, 4649, 4610
4 (a) 40 (b) 15 (c) 58 (d) 33 (e) 97
5 (a) 1300 (b) 1660 (c) 1535 (d) 1313
  (e) 982
6 (a) 210 (b) 70 (c) 222
  (d) 272 (e) 38
7 (a) 3961 (b) 39 660 (c) 13 966
8 (a) 12 (b) 73 (c) 387 (d) 31 (e) 63 (f) 2378
9 96   10 141   11 83   12 121
13 122   14 115   15 142   16 209
17 686   18 923   19 1240   20 1540
21 6500   22 8300   23 9100   24 44
25 59   26 28   27 17   28 38
29 350   30 190   31 213   32 585
33 275   34 626   35 2200   36 2900

2 Multiplying and dividing mentally by single digits and powers of 10

1 (a) 20 (b) 200 (c) 2000 (d) 2000
2 (a) 48 (b) 480 (c) 4800 (d) 48 000
3 (a) 350 (b) 160 (c) 240 (d) 6400 (e) 2100
  (f) 4900 (g) 360 000 (h) 300 000
4 (a) 8 (b) 27 (c) 450 (d) 538
  (e) 13 (f) 138 (g) 10 (h) 40
5 (a) 6 (b) 6 (c) 300 (d) 3
6 (a) 7 (b) 90 (c) 7 (d) 900
7 (a) 50 (b) 50 (c) 90 (d) 60 (e) 90
  (f) 300 (g) 9 (h) 500
8 (a) 4900 (b) 500 (c) 48 000 (d) 60
  (e) 100 000 (f) 1 (g) 3200 (h) 200
  (i) 4900 (j) 80

3 Multiplying whole numbers

1 777   2 1197   3 858   4 864
5 1431   6 1872   7 3876   8 6853
9 1725   10 2072   11 8280   12 2376
13 17 936 14 23 923 15 60 120 16 45 738
17 59 166 18 129 833 19 333 032 20 119 119

4 Dividing whole numbers

1 58   2 27   3 49   4 68
5 26   6 35   7 24   8 32
9 26   10 43   11 78   12 43
13 9 r 2 or $9\frac{2}{3}$ or 9.7   14 10 r 3 or $10\frac{3}{5}$ or 10.6
15 9 r 6 or $9\frac{6}{7}$ or 9.9   16 8 r 4 or $8\frac{4}{12}$ or $8\frac{1}{3}$ or 8.3
17 5 r 5 or $5\frac{5}{17}$ or 5.3   18 8 r 16 or $8\frac{16}{23}$ or 8.7
19 10 r 33 or $10\frac{33}{39}$ or 10.8 20 36 r 13 or $36\frac{13}{71}$ or 36.2

5 Selecting the correct operation to solve problems

1 £858   2 9 weeks (£31.50)   3 36 000
4 19 bags 5 34p   6 £903
7 £235 = 275 francs. So cheaper in England.
8 11 cm
9 (a) (i) $6 + 5 - 4 = 7$ (ii) $4 + 5 - 6 = 3$
  (b) (i) $65 + 4 = 69$ (ii) $45 + 6 = 51$
  (c) (i) $65 - 4 = 61$ (ii) $45 - 6 = 39$
  (d) (i) $54 \times 6 = 324$ (ii) $56 \times 4 = 224$
  (e) (i) $6 \times 5 - 4 = 26$ (ii) $4 \times 5 - 6 = 14$
  (f) (i) $6 \times 5 + 4 = 34$ (ii) $4 \times 5 + 6 = 26$
10 (a) $34 + 57 + 68$ (b) $35 + 4 + 6 - 7 - 8$
   (c) $456 \times 3 + 7 - 8$ (d) $3 \times 7 + 4 \times 8 + 5 \times 6$
   (e) $87 - 34 + 6 - 5$ (f) $3 \times 8 + 6 \times 4 - 7 - 5$

6 Negative numbers 1

1 (a) –4 (b) –9 (c) –9 (d) –17
2 (a) 4 (b) –3 (c) 9 (d) 15
3 (a) 6 (b) 12 (c) –2 (d) 0 (e) –2 (f) 1
  (g) –13 (h) –5 (i) –10 (j) –4 (k) 1 (l) –16
  (m) 15 (n) 14
4 (a) –11 (b) –6 (c) –33 (d) –7 (e) 47
  (f) –31 (g) 0 (h) 75 (i) –17 (j) 6 (k) 13
  (l) –28 (m) –16 (n) –58 (o) 0 (p) 0
5 (a) –2 (b) 24

7 Negative numbers 2

1 (a) 24 (b) –35 (c) –18 (d) 32 (e) 36
  (f) 28 (g) 0 (h) 0 (i) –24 (j) 28
  (k) –27 (l) 11
2 (a) –4 (b) 6 (c) 4 (d) –1 (e) –2 (f) –4
  (g) 0 (h) 8 (i) –9 (j) 8 (k) –3 (l) –1
3 (a) –4 (b) –24 (c) –30 (d) 7 (e) 27
  (f) 16 (g) 9 (h) –4 (i) –5 (j) –1
  (k) –6 (l) –1
4 (a) 18 (b) –32 (c) 14 (d) –18 (e) 2
  (f) –4 (g) –7 (h) 2 (i) 7 (j) –29

8 Order of operations

1 (a) 50 (b) 22 (c) 16 (d) 10
2 (a) 3 (b) 59 (c) 71 (d) –45
3 (a) 9 (b) –56 (c) 23 (d) 17
4 (a) 20 (b) 23 (c) –50 (d) 37 (e) 17 (f) –27
5 (a) –7 (b) 133 (c) –42 (d) –425
6 (a) –2 (b) –1 (c) –5 (d) –1
7 (a) $4 \times 5 - 3 \times (8 - 7) - 2 = 15$
  (b) $4 \times (5 - 3) \times 8 - 7 - 2 = 55$
  (c) $4 \times 5 - 3 \times (8 - (7 - 2)) = 11$
  (d) $4 \times (5 - 3 \times 8) - 7 - 2 = -85$

9 Factors and divisibility tests

1 (a) 351, 756, 747, 594 (b) 732, 756, 858, 594
2 (a) 324, 276, 788 (b) 243, 324, 276, 987
(c) 324, 276
3 (a) Ends in 0 or 5; digits add to a multiple of 3.
(b) 75, 735, 1230, 1305, 12 345
4 144, 624, 768
5 2, 3, 5, 7, 11, 13, 17, 19, 23, 29, 31, 37, 41, 43, 47, 53, 59, 61, 67, 71, 73, 79, 83, 89, 97
6 1, 4, 9, 16, 25, 36, 49, 64, 81, 100
7 4, 9, 25, 49, squares of primes
8 (a) (i) 6 (ii) 12 (iii) 24 (iv) 48 (v) 60 (b) 192
(If the doubling pattern observed as far as (a)(iv) had continued we would get 96 and then 192.)
The 14 factors are 1, 2, 3, 4, 6, 8, 112, 16, 24, 32, 48, 64, 96 and 192.

10 Primes, squares, square roots and cubes

1 (a) 29, 89 (b) 4, 9, 49, 64 (c) 64
2 (a) 49 (b) 121 (c) 196 (d) 9 (e) 12 (f) 13
(g) 64 (h) 343 (i) 729 (j) 3 (k) 10 (l) 5
3 (a) Divisible by 3 $(5 + 7 = 12)$
(b) Divisible by 3 $(1 + 4 + 5 + 2 = 12)$
(c) Divisible by 5 (ends in 5)
(d) $7 \times 13 = 91$ (e) $11 \times 13 = 143$
(f) Divisible by 9 $(3 + 4 + 8 + 3 = 18)$
4 (a) 289 (b) Because 17 is the next biggest prime after 13 and $17^2 = 289 > 211$ (c) Clearly not divisible by 2 or 5. Digit sum is 4, so not divisible by 3. Not divisible by 7, 11 or 13 (check by dividing).
5 223, 227, 229

11 Prime factorisation

1 (a) $2^2 \times 5$ (b) $2^3 \times 5$ (c) 3^4 (d) $3 \times 5 \times 7$
(e) $2 \times 7 \times 17$ (f) $3 \times 7 \times 11$ (g) $2^5 \times 3$
(h) $3 \times 7 \times 13$
2 (a) $6 = 2 \times 3, 16 = 2^4; 2^4 \times 3 = 48$
(b) $8 = 2^3, 18 = 2 \times 3^2; 2^3 \times 3^2 = 72$
(c) $21 = 3 \times 7, 35 = 5 \times 7; 3 \times 5 \times 7 = 105$
(d) $84 = 2^3 \times 3 \times 7, 147 = 3 \times 7^2; 2^2 \times 3 \times 7^2 = 588$
(e) $18 = 2 \times 3^2, 30 = 2 \times 3 \times 5; 2 \times 3^2 \times 5 = 90$
(f) $45 = 3^2 \times 5, 75 = 3 \times 5^2; 3^2 \times 5^2 = 225$
3 (a) $24 = 2^3 \times 3, 80 = 2^4 \times 5; 2^3 = 8$
(b) $56 = 2^3 \times 7, 84 = 2^2 \times 3 \times 7; 2^2 \times 7 = 28$
(c) $42 = 2 \times 3 \times 7, 70 = 2 \times 5 \times 7; 2 \times 7 = 14$
(d) $60 = 2^2 \times 3 \times 5, 96 = 2^5 \times 3; 2^2 \times 3 = 12$
(e) $567 = 3^4 \times 7, 729 = 3^6; 3^4 = 81$
(f) $147 = 3 \times 7^2, 343 = 7^3; 7^2 = 49$
4 (a) 2 (b) 16 (c) 18 (d) 25 $(= 3^2 + 4^2)$
5 (a) $2^2 \times 3^3 \times 7$
(b) $3 \times 7 = 21$ (The number is $2^2 \times 3^4 \times 7^2 = 15\,876 = 126^2$)
6 (a) $2^2 \times 3 \times 5^2 \times 7^2$
(b) $2^2 \times 3^2 \times 5^2 \times 7^2 = 44\,100 = 210^2$ (3 times 14 700)

12 Fractions of quantities

1 (a) £9 (b) £13 (c) £16 (d) £65
2 (a) 30 (b) 100 (c) 12 (d) 30 (e) 18 (f) 48
3 (a) 39 (b) 27 (c) 35 (d) 135 (e) 65
(f) 240 (g) 1500
4 18   5 90   6 30   7 $\frac{5}{12}$
8 1000 people   9 15 sweets   10 18 males

11 (a) 63 (b) 60 (c) Hamster (d) $\frac{3}{4}$
12 (a) 20 (b) 21 (c) 30 (d) 42 (e) 96 (f) 119
13 $\frac{480}{800} = \frac{3}{5}$

13 Equivalent fractions and ordering fractions

1 e.g. $\frac{2}{7} = \frac{4}{14} = \frac{6}{21} = \frac{10}{35} = \frac{20}{70} = \frac{200}{700}\cdots$
2 $\frac{5}{6} = \frac{15}{18} = \frac{20}{24} = \frac{50}{60} = \frac{45}{54} = \frac{60}{72} = \frac{100}{120}; \frac{3}{5} = \frac{12}{20} = \frac{15}{25} = \frac{21}{35} = \frac{60}{100};$
$\frac{24}{30} \left(= \frac{4}{5}\right)$ is the odd one out.
3 (a) $\frac{1}{4}$ (b) $\frac{3}{4}$ (c) $\frac{5}{8}$ (d) $\frac{5}{12}$
4 $\frac{450}{3000} = \frac{3}{20}$
5 (a) $\frac{135}{360} = \frac{3}{8}$ (b) $\frac{5}{6}$ of 3 hours = $2\frac{1}{2}$ hours
6 (a) < (b) < (c) < (d) = (e) >
(f) > (g) = (h) < (i) <
7 $\frac{1}{7}, \frac{2}{8}, \frac{2}{7}, \frac{3}{9}, \frac{3}{8}, \frac{4}{9}$
8 (a) $\frac{1}{4}, \frac{5}{16}, \frac{3}{8}$ (b) $\frac{4}{5}, \frac{7}{8}, \frac{9}{10}$ (c) $\frac{2}{7}, \frac{3}{10}, \frac{1}{3}$
9 (a) $\frac{5}{6}$ (b) e.g. $\frac{49}{60}$ 10 e.g. $\frac{1}{100.5} = \frac{2}{201}$

14 Using and ordering decimals

1 (a) 150 (b) 8.5 (c) 99.5 (d) 2.35
(e) 6.6 (f) 5.55 (g) 5.95 (h) 3.85
2 (a) (i) 8.9 (ii) 8.0 (iii) 43.2 (iv) 20.1
(b) (i) 7.03 (ii) 6.00 (iii) 4.02 (iv) 4.06
(c) (i) 5.8 (ii) 7.9 (iii) 9.9 (iv) 3.65
(d) (i) 4.28 (ii) 2.08 (iii) 8.98 (iv) 4.99
3 (a) (i) 4 (ii) 1 (iii) 23
(b) (i) 9 (ii) 91 (iii) 80
(c) (i) 73 (ii) 60 (iii) 500
(d) (i) 543 (ii) 620 (iii) 1000
4 (a) (i) 236p (ii) 450p (iii) 2000p
(b) (i) 200 cm (ii) 230 cm (iii) 178 cm
(c) (i) 3000 g (ii) 4328 g (iii) 600 g
(d) (i) 4 m (ii) 2.53 m (iii) 0.2 m
5 (a) 5.5, 5.8, 6.3, 6.9   (b) 0.12, 0.16, 0.4, 0.8
(c) 5.699, 5.729, 5.73, 57.2
(d) 0.0101, 0.101, 0.11, 1.1001

15 Equivalence of fractions and decimals 1

1 (a) 0.4 (b) 0.37 (c) 0.15 (d) 0.09 (e) 0.001
2 (a) 1.2 (b) 3.75 (c) 8.7 (d) 0.125
(e) 4.375 (f) 7.22 (g) 2.65 (h) 6.8125
3 (a) $\frac{3}{5} = 0.6, \frac{5}{8} = 0.625, \frac{4}{5} = 0.8, \frac{1}{2} = 0.5, \frac{3}{4} = 0.75$
(b) $\frac{1}{2}, \frac{3}{5}, \frac{5}{8}, \frac{3}{4}, \frac{4}{5}$
4 (a) $\frac{2}{5}$ (b) $\frac{4}{5}$ (c) $2\frac{1}{4}$ (d) $3\frac{3}{20}$ (e) $4\frac{14}{25}$
(f) $\frac{1}{8}$ (g) $7\frac{5}{8}$ (h) $\frac{3}{1000}$ (i) $\frac{1}{125}$
5 (a) $\frac{1}{25}$ (b) $\frac{7}{50}$ (c) $\frac{6}{25}$ (d) $\frac{17}{50}$ (e) $\frac{11}{25}$
(f) $\frac{27}{50}$ (g) $\frac{16}{25}$ (h) $\frac{37}{50}$ (i) $\frac{21}{25}$

16 Equivalence of fractions and decimals 2

1 (a) 0.3̇; recurs (b) 0.75 (c) 0.4 (d) 0.16̇; recurs
  (e) 0.4̇28 571̇; recurs (f) 0.375 (g) 0.5̇; recurs
  (h) 0.3 (i) 0.6̇3̇; recurs (j) 0.916̇; recurs

2 (a) terminates (b) recurs (c) terminates
  (d) recurs (e) terminates (f) terminates
  (g) recurs (h) recurs (i) terminates (j) recurs

3 (a) terminates $\left(=\frac{1}{2}\right)$ (b) terminates $\left(=\frac{3}{4}\right)$
  (c) recurs $\left(=\frac{5}{6}\right)$ (d) recurs $\left(=\frac{2}{3}\right)$
  (e) terminates $\left(=\frac{3}{8}\right)$ (f) terminates $\left(=\frac{3}{10}\right)$

4 (a) $\frac{1}{13}=0.0̇76 923̇$ $\frac{2}{13}=0.1̇53 846̇$ $\frac{3}{13}=0.2̇30 769̇$
  $\frac{4}{13}=0.3̇07 692̇$ $\frac{5}{13}=0.3̇84 615̇$ $\frac{6}{13}=0.4̇61 538̇$
  $\frac{7}{13}=0.5̇38 461̇$ $\frac{8}{13}=0.6̇15 384̇$ $\frac{9}{13}=0.6̇92 307̇$
  $\frac{10}{13}=0.7̇69 230̇$ $\frac{11}{13}=0.8̇46 153̇$ $\frac{12}{13}=0.9̇23 076̇$

(b)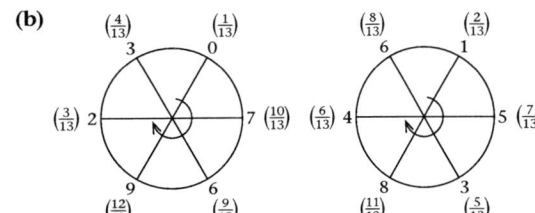

17 Multiplying and dividing decimal numbers

1 0.16	2 0.9	3 10.5	4 32.5
5 0.28	6 23	7 600	8 850
9 480	10 0.49	11 1.44	12 0.0064
13 5.76	14 14.44	15 23.94	16 4.5
17 4.25	18 120	19 50	20 3
21 3.5	22 0.2	23 20	24 20
25 1.85	26 4.8	27 7200	28 0.78
29 4.78	30 0.29		

18 The four rules of decimals

1 22.75	2 2.38	3 10.05	4 0.539
5 55.97	6 5.5	7 6.288	8 49.302
9 9	10 0.105	11 100	12 0.28
13 3.99	14 32.3	15 72.66	16 22.09
17 4.25	18 50	19 3.5	20 2.4
21 0.003	22 63	23 0.8	24 28.09
25 4.32	26 580	27 142.86	28 0.61
29 5.19	30 0.09		

19 Fractions, decimals and percentages

1 (a) 0.17 (b) 0.78 (c) 0.06 (d) 0.003
2 (a) $\frac{3}{4}$ (b) $\frac{4}{5}$ (c) $\frac{3}{50}$ (d) $\frac{1}{200}$
3 (a) 74% (b) 70% (c) 65% (d) 22.5%

4

Fraction	Decimal	Percentage
$\frac{4}{5}$	0.8	80%
$\frac{1}{3}$	0.3̇	$33\frac{1}{3}$%
$\frac{9}{20}$	0.45	45%
$\frac{1}{8}$	0.125	12.5%
$\frac{6}{25}$	0.24	24%
$\frac{2}{25}$	0.08	8%

5 Sean (Sean $66\frac{2}{3}$%, Shardi 65%, Tracey 60%)
6 Fizzy Fitness (Fizzy Fitness: $\frac{2}{5}$ = 40%;
  Endless Exercise: 100% − 65% = 35%;
  Wacky Workout: $\frac{3}{8}$ = 37.5%)

7 (a) 0.375, $\frac{3}{8}$ (b) 0.035, $\frac{7}{200}$ (c) 0.16̇, $\frac{1}{6}$

8 22%, 0.227, $\frac{7}{27}$ (= 0.2̇59̇), 27%, $\frac{2}{7}$ (= 0.2̇85 714̇),
  $\frac{7}{22}$ (= 0.31̇8̇), 77%, $2\frac{2}{7}$ (= 2.2̇85 714̇), 2.7,
  $\frac{22}{7}$ (= 3.1̇42 857̇)

9 $\frac{5}{13}$ (38%), $\frac{11}{27}$ (41%), $\frac{13}{31}$ (42%), $\frac{11}{24}$ (46%),
  $\frac{8}{17}$ (47%), $\frac{25}{52}$ (48%)

20 Finding percentages without a calculator

1 (a) 12 (b) 63 (c) 34 (d) 5.2 (e) 24 (f) 48
2 (a) 4 (b) 9 (c) 35 (d) 4 (e) 3
3 (a) £96 (b) £5.85 (c) £5.58 (d) £910 (e) £315
  (f) £103.50 (g) £42 (h) £280 (i) £2.01
4 (a) 99p (b) £14.30
5 (a) £24.65 (b) £55.25
6 (a) 50 (b) 1420 (c) 40.5
7 (a) 100 (b) 180 (c) 115
8 (a) £84.60 (b) £98.70 (c) £411.25
  (d) £928.25 (e) £17 390

21 Finding percentages with a calculator

1 (a) £240.50 (b) 20.4 km (c) £104.83 (d) £35.10
2 Electric Power: £119; Supersaver £113.33
3

Percentage change	Multiplier
Increase by 5%	× 1.05
Decrease by 8%	× 0.92
Decrease by 25%	× 0.75
Increase by 20%	× 1.2
Increase by 50%	× 1.5
Decrease by 34%	× 0.66
Decrease by 10%	× 0.90
Decrease by 12.5%	× 0.875
Increase by 100%	× 2

4 (a) £66 (b) £80.64 (c) £46.20 (d) £69.70
  (e) £230.10 (f) £29.90
5 £28.45 + 260 × 12.5p = £60.95
  £60.95 + VAT = £71.61 (rounding down to nearest p,
  which is convention for VAT)

22 Finding one quantity as a percentage of another

1 52%
2 (a) 48% (b) 65%
3 (a) 58% (b) 72% (c) 58%
4 Keep Going Somehow (8 out of 10 is 80%)
5 Women (27% compared with 25%)
6 Gaddesby United (78% compared with 68%)
7 CD player (15% compared with 13%)
8 No (men 44%, women 52%)

23 Repeated percentage change

1 £526.68 **(b)** Decreased by 7.6% (or 8%)
2 £9560 **3 (a)** £61.80 **(b)** $1.07^3 = 1.225\,043$
4 (a) £12 300 (£12 320) **(b)** £4500 (£4459.39)
5 (a) $14.52\ \text{cm}^2$ **(b)** 21% **6 (a)** £5.32 **(b)** 44%
7 6.3% increase **8** 7.7% decrease

24 Reverse percentages

1 (a) £25 **(b)** £265 **2 (a)** £50 **(b)** £9
3 440 ml **4 (a)** £10 **(b)** £10.50
5 Vitamin C 60 mg, Iron 14.4 mg, Riboflavin 1.5 mg,
Thiamin 1.3 mg
6 1550 **7** £12 500 **8** £14 400
9 £15.48 or £15.49
10 Shoes £41.70, Shirt £12.77, Coat £72.34, Socks £3.66

25 Rounding numbers

1 9000, 265 000, 1 477 000
2 (a) 6.39 **(b)** 47.64 **(c)** 8.56 **(d)** 78.10
3 (a) 0.04 **(b)** 74.65 **(c)** 500.00 **(d)** 0.00
(e) 63.02 **(f)** 20.00
4 (a) 688 000 **(b)** 0.004 99 **(c)** 300 **(d)** 339
(e) 775 000 **(f)** 10.0
5 (a) 649 **(b)** 648.8 **(c)** 650 **(d)** 648.791 **(e)** 649
6 (a) 8520 **(b)** 8500 **(c)** 9000 **(d)** 8519.0
7 (a) 3.48 **(b)** 49.08 **(c)** 27.90 **(d)** 7.56
8 (a) 30 000 people **(b)** 50 kg **(c)** 500 m
(d) 30 000 million gallons
9 (a) 28 000 people **(b)** 46 kg **(c)** 450 m
(d) 27 000 million gallons **(e)** 5.7 miles
(f) 0.00048 m
10 (a) 24.5 cm, 23.5 cm **(b)** 40.5 cm, 39.5 cm
(c) 3.45 cm, 3.35 cm **(d)** 5.05 cm, 4.95 cm
(e) 100.5 m, 99.5 m **(f)** 435 km, 425 km

26 Estimation and efficient use of a calculator

1 (a) $400 \times 20 = 8000$ **(b)** $900 \div 30 = 30$
(c) $4 \times 0.5 = 2$ **(d)** $0.8 \div 0.2 = 4$
(e) $\sqrt{(9+16)} = \sqrt{25} = 5$ **(f)** $\frac{6}{12} + \frac{28}{56} = \frac{1}{2} + \frac{1}{2} = 1$
2 (a) $500 \times 2 = 1000$ **(b)** $400 \div 20 = 20$
(c) $(18 \times 3) \div 6 = \frac{54}{6} = 9$
(d) $\sqrt{(2^3 + 2^3)} = \sqrt{(8+8)} = \sqrt{16} = 4$
(e) $(6+4) \div (1+4) = \frac{10}{5} = 2$
(f) $3^3 \div (14-5) = \frac{27}{9} = 3$
3 *Question 1* **(a)** 7540 **(b)** 31.5 **(c)** 1.99 **(d)** 4.04
(e) 5.27 **(f)** 0.957
Question 2 **(a)** 1020 **(b)** 15.3 **(c)** 9.54 **(d)** 3.99
(e) 2.00 **(f)** 2.77
4 3000 million seconds ($60 \times 60 \times 20 \times 400 \times 100$ is a
good enough estimate)

27 Trial and improvement

1 3.42 cm **2** 7.6 and 10.6 **3** 3.7
4 23.4 **5** 6.8 cm **6** 1953.125 and 4492.125

28 Time

1

	1998	1999	2000	2001	2002	2003
25th December	Fri	Sat	Mon	Tues	Wed	Thurs
14th February	Sat	Sun	Mon	Wed	Thurs	Fri

2 (a) 45 mins **(b)** 3 hrs 45 mins **(c)** 5 hrs 20 mins
(d) 3 hrs 50 mins

3

Departure time	Travelling time (mins)	Arrival time
11:15	26	**11:41**
12:46	**17**	13:03
14:25	37	**15:02**
12:55	55	13:50

4 (a) 11.28 a.m. or 11.48 a.m.; arrives only 4 minutes
under the 5 hours **(b)** 17:46 **(c)** 18:32

5

Hours and minutes	Hours	Minutes
2 hours 30 minutes	2.5	150
2 hours 45 minutes	2.75	165
2 hours 24 minutes	2.4	144
1 hour 40 minutes	1.67	100
5 hours 20 minutes	5.33	320
3 hours 51 minutes	3.85	231

6 (a) 5 hrs 22 mins **(b)** 2 hrs 50 mins
(c) 7 hrs 43 mins

29 Speed

1 3 mph **2** 50 miles **3** 1 mile
4 $2\frac{1}{2}$ hours **5** 1 hour 40 minutes
6 (a) (i) 75 miles **(ii)** 10 miles **(iii)** $2\frac{1}{2}$ miles
(b) (i) 5 hours **(ii)** $1\frac{1}{2}$ hours **(iii)** 2 minutes
7 (a) 24 mph **(b)** 32 miles
8 (a) 64 mph **(b)** 56 mph
9 (a) 576 mph **(b)** $768\ \text{km}^2$
10 (a) 8 mins 20 secs, 16 mins 40 secs
(b) 3.6 km, 1.8 km

30 Ratio

1 2600
2 (a) $\frac{1}{3}$ (16 out of 48) **(b)** 1 : 2
(c) 4 more (ratio 20 : 28)
3 (a) 1 : 3 **(b)** 1 : 5 **(c)** 3 : 4 **(d)** 1 : 3
(e) 1 : 3 **(f)** 2 : 3
4 £90, £120, £150
5 140 men
6 (a) 20 cm **(b)** 12 cm
7 (a) 160 g **(b)** 750 g **(c)** 5 : 4
8 (a) 24.5 cm **(b)** 24 cm

31 Direct proportion

1 (a) £3.50 (b) £17.50 (c) £10.50
2 (a) 65p (b) £1.95 (c) £3.25
3 (a) £6.40 (b) £19.20 (c) £76.80
4 £7 **5** £46 **6** £1.26 **7** 15 minutes
8 (a) 4 (b) 0 (c) 8
9 $3\frac{1}{2}$ pounds
10 (a) 386 miles (b) 313 miles
11 9-pack (In 4-pack each roll costs 41p; in 9-pack each roll costs 37p.)
12 500 g bag (500 g costs 0.15p per g; 850 g costs 0.16p per g. Or, in 500 g bag you get 6.7 g for 1p; in 850 g bag you get 6.3 g for 1p.)
13 Same (One window costs £285 for both firms.)

32 Indices

1 (a) 1 (b) 1 (c) 1 (d) 4 (e) 15 (f) 1
(g) 2 (h) 1 (i) 2
2 (a) $\frac{1}{3}$ (b) $\frac{1}{6}$ (c) $\frac{1}{16}$ (d) $\frac{1}{16}$ (e) $\frac{1}{100}$ (f) $\frac{1}{32}$
(g) $\frac{1}{49}$ (h) $\frac{1}{9}$ (i) $\frac{1}{216}$ (j) 1 (k) 3 (l) $2\frac{1}{2}$
(m) 8 (n) $2\frac{1}{4}$ (o) 0.769
3 (a) $\frac{1}{8}$ (b) $\frac{1}{6}$ (c) $\frac{1}{53}$ (d) 1
4 (a) $7\frac{1}{2}$ (b) $1\frac{2}{3}$ (c) $1\frac{1}{5}$ (d) $2\frac{2}{5}$
5 (a) $\frac{4}{11}$ (b) $\frac{3}{22}$ (c) $\frac{3}{7}$ (d) $\frac{7}{22}$
6 (a) 2.5 (b) 4 (c) 0.8 (d) 0.625

33 Using indices

1 (a) 3^6 (b) 5^6 (c) 6^3 (d) 7^{12}
2 (a) 2^1 (b) 3^{-2} (c) 5^2 (d) 7^{-3}
3 (a) 49 (b) 0.25
4 (a) $3^2 \div 3^3 \times 3^4 = 3^3$ (b) $5^2 \times 5^3 \times 5^4 = 5^9$
(c) $5^{-2} \times 5^{-3} = 5^{-5}$ (d) $3^5 \times 3^{-4} \times 3^{-4} = 3^{-3}$
5 (a) 5 (b) 3 (c) 3 (d) −3
6 (a) 5 (b) 7 (c) 3 (d) −2
7 (a) $a = 5, b = 5$ (b) $a = 6, b = 6$ (c) $a = -8, b = 5$

34 Standard form

1 (a) 23 500 (b) 3 576 000 (c) 243 100
(d) 4 235 600 000 000 (e) 6 380 000 000 000 000
(f) 0.000 641 (g) 0.000 002 538
(h) 0.000 010 54 (i) 0.000 000 075 2
2 (a) 6.462×10^3 (b) 4.32×10^4
(c) 3.42×10^8 (d) 4.5312×10^6 (e) 3.2×10^{-4}
(f) 2.34×10^{14} (g) 7.23×10^{-5} (h) 2.37×10^{-5}
(i) 8.1×10^{-3}
3 (a) 4×10^3 (b) 7×10^2 (c) 6×10^6 (d) 1.25×10^7
4 9.935×10^6, 3.467×10^8, 3.5×10^8, 4.62×10^8,
6.9312×10^9, 1.1×10^{11}
5 0, 9.9×10^{-3}, 3.72×10^{-2}, 0.389, 5.23×10^{-1}, 0.58, 1,
4.0005, 1.42×10^2

35 Standard form with a calculator

1 (a) 1.94×10^{11} (b) 2.27×10^4 (c) 8.29×10^5
(d) 6.14×10^{-8} (e) 4.45×10^{-10} (f) 1.68×10^{-5}
(g) 2×10^{-14} (h) 1.62×10^{15} (i) 7.52×10^7
(j) 7.51×10^7 (k) 8.89×10^8 (l) 5.52×10^6
2 15 years in seconds is about 4.73×10^8; 16 years in seconds is about 5.05×10^8

3 (a) 1.14×10^9 litres (b) 4.16×10^{11} litres
4 299 800 km per second × 2595 seconds
= 7.78×10^8 km
5 (a) 2.86×10^9 cans or 3×10^9 cans, more sensibly (b) 50 cans each

36 Standard form without a calculator

1 7.5×10^7 **2** 1.4×10^6 **3** 2.87×10^9
4 7.2×10^{10} **5** 2.15×10^6 **6** 4×10^{10}
7 8.1×10^7 **8** 3×10^3 **9** 5×10^3
10 7.2×10^4 **11** 5×10^5 **12** 7.5×10^2
13 9.5×10^9 **14** 2.05×10^6 **15** 1.177×10^7
16 5.215×10^7 **17** 7.9195×10^{11} **18** 8×10^3
19 3.6×10^{-3} **20** 7×10^2

37 Adding and subtracting simple fractions

1 $\frac{7}{8}$ **2** $\frac{1}{6}$ **3** $\frac{5}{12}$ **4** $\frac{1}{10}$ **5** $\frac{11}{12}$
6 $\frac{4}{12} = \frac{1}{3}$ **7** 1 **8** $1\frac{1}{4}$ **9** $\frac{1}{12}$ **10** $\frac{19}{12} = 1\frac{7}{12}$
11 $\frac{20}{36} = \frac{5}{9}$ **12** $\frac{14}{15}$ **13** $1\frac{1}{9}$ **14** $\frac{10}{15} = \frac{2}{3}$ **15** $\frac{31}{24} = 1\frac{7}{24}$
16 $\frac{5}{24}$ **17** $\frac{13}{18}$ **18** $\frac{23}{30}$ **19** $\frac{1}{30}$ **20** $\frac{41}{40} = 1\frac{1}{40}$
21 $\frac{11}{40}$ **22** $\frac{1}{8}$ **23** $1\frac{3}{4}$ **24** $4\frac{1}{3}$ **25** $3\frac{3}{4}$
26 $2\frac{1}{4}$ **27** $1\frac{3}{4}$ **28** $\frac{17}{12} = 1\frac{5}{12}$ **29** $\frac{5}{8}$ **30** $\frac{1}{12}$

38 Multiplying and dividing simple fractions

1 $\frac{3}{20}$ **2** $\frac{5}{24}$ **3** $\frac{1}{24}$ **4** $\frac{3}{25}$ **5** $\frac{1}{6}$
6 $\frac{5}{16}$ **7** $\frac{1}{3}$ **8** $\frac{1}{6}$ **9** $\frac{2}{5}$ **10** $\frac{1}{2}$
11 8 **12** 6 **13** 5 **14** 12 **15** 12
16 $\frac{2}{5}$ **17** $\frac{3}{10}$ **18** $\frac{1}{10}$ **19** $\frac{1}{12}$ **20** 2
21 3 **22** $2\frac{1}{2}$ **23** $1\frac{1}{3}$ **24** $1\frac{1}{4}$ **25** $1\frac{1}{3}$
26 $2\frac{1}{2}$ **27** $\frac{9}{14}$ **28** 2 **29** $\frac{1}{2}$ **30** $4\frac{1}{2}$

39 The four rules of fractions

1 $8\frac{5}{12}$ **2** $6\frac{1}{2}$ **3** $14\frac{1}{6}$ **4** $3\frac{1}{3}$ **5** $3\frac{1}{2}$
6 $\frac{11}{12}$ **7** 10 **8** $4\frac{5}{12}$ **9** 6 **10** $14\frac{2}{3}$
11 1 **12** 4 **13** $2\frac{3}{10}$ **14** $8\frac{8}{15}$ **15** $1\frac{13}{32}$
16 42 **17** $6\frac{1}{12}$ miles **18** $33\frac{3}{4}$ litres
19 $\frac{2}{3}$ minute = 40 seconds **20** $9\frac{5}{8}$ pints

40 Square roots and surds

1 (a) 3 (b) 7 (c) 30 (d) 50 (e) 110 (f) 200
2 (a) 15 (b) 21 (c) 32 (d) 27 (e) 36 (f) 105
3 (a) 0.2 (b) 0.6 (c) 0.4 (d) 0.05
(e) 0.12 (f) 0.14
4 (a) $7\sqrt{5}$ (b) $5\sqrt{11}$ (c) $4\sqrt{10}$ (d) $4\sqrt{3}$
(e) $\sqrt{2}$ (f) 0
5 (a) $6\sqrt{3}$ (b) $5\sqrt{5}$ (c) $6\sqrt{5}$ (d) $2\sqrt{2}$
(e) $4\sqrt{3}$ (f) $\sqrt{7}$
6 (a) $5\sqrt{5}$ (b) $5\sqrt{7}$ (c) $7\sqrt{6}$ (d) $\sqrt{10}$
(e) $\sqrt{11}$ (f) $3\sqrt{7}$
7 (a) 10 (b) 7 (c) 12 (d) 45